ROAD TRIP!

ROAD TRIP!

The Sports Lover's Travel Guide to Museums, Halls of Fame, Fantasy Camps, Stadium Tours, and More!

LISA IANNUCCI

GUILFORD, CONNECTICUT

An imprint of The Rowman & Littlefield Publishing Group, Inc.
4501 Forbes Blvd., Ste. 200
Lanham, MD 20706
www.rowman.com

Distributed by NATIONAL BOOK NETWORK

British Library Cataloguing in Publication Information available

Library of Congress Cataloging-in-Publication Data available

Names: Iannucci, Lisa, author.
Title: Road trip : the sports lover's travel guide to museums, halls of fame, fantasy camps, stadium tours, and more! / Lisa Iannucci.
Description: Guilford, Connecticut : Lyons Press, 2020. | Includes index. | Summary: "This guidebook breaks down—state by state-every place a sports fan will want to visit. Included are restaurants owned by sports celebrities and new sites. Also features celebrity cruises with sports teams, birthplaces and grave sites of star athletes, and more obscure museums"— Provided by publisher.
Identifiers: LCCN 2019046325 (print) | LCCN 2019046326 (ebook) | ISBN 9781493044573 (paperback) | ISBN 9781493044580 (epub)
Subjects: LCSH: Sports—United States—Guidebooks. | Sports tourism—United States—Guidebooks.
Classification: LCC GV583 .I37 2020 (print) | LCC GV583 (ebook) | DDC 796.0973—dc23
LC record available at https://lccn.loc.gov/2019046325
LC ebook record available at https://lccn.loc.gov/2019046326

♾™ The paper used in this publication meets the minimum requirements of American National Standard for Information Sciences—Permanence of Paper for Printed Library Materials, ANSI/NISO Z39.48-1992

Unless otherwise noted, senior prices apply to those 65 and older.

If an attraction description does not mention tours, please assume they are not available. Always call ahead to verify hours and tour availability.

CONTENTS

ACKNOWLEDGMENTS

There are so many people who help you to write a book. They don't actually write the book for you, but they believe in you, inspire you to keep going when you're tired from writing hours on end, lend you their expertise, help you with small details, and keep you on track. That's what my circle does for me, and for that I'm a better writer.

Let's start with acknowledging Rick Rinehart, my editor at Globe Pequot, who believed in this book. Thank you, Rick, for always loving my ideas. Thanks also to production editor Meredith Dias and copy editor Joshua Rosenberg (who really knows his sports!). To my children (who are now incredible adults)—Nicole, Travis, and Samantha—who are now, and always will be, my life. In everything I do all three of you light my way to the end. To my mom, Patricia Quaglieri, because there isn't a book in my career that I haven't thanked her for, and this one isn't going to be any different. She always supports and loves me. Love you too, Mom. To my honey, Ej "The Rainmaker" Garr—thank you for your love and your support, and for answering all of my sports questions because you are a sports trivia master. I couldn't do what I do without any of you.

INTRODUCTION

As I finish writing this book, it's March Madness, 2019. It's what every college basketball team fights to get to every year.

I'm watching the Duke University Blue Devils versus the Louisiana State University (LSU) Tigers on television. The Blue Devils are one of the teams favored to win the entire tournament. LSU came into the tournament as underdogs, but they are not playing like it. Instead, they give Duke a run for their money, nearly knocking them out of contention.

The game literally comes down to the last second. Two LSU layups circle the rim but don't fall through. LSU loses by one point and their players collapse on the court, overwhelmed with emotion because they missed their chance to get to the Sweet 16. They fought hard—really hard—but Duke advanced. Watching at home, I screamed at incredible three-pointers, slam dunks, and blocked shots. I felt crushed for the Tigers and excited for the Blue Devils all at the same time.

College hoops brings so much adrenaline to the court, it's crazy.

Actually, sports as a whole is very exciting, but if you're holding this book you're a sports fan and you already know that. When I was a young girl, I was obsessed with the New York Mets (and their infielder Doug Flynn to be honest). I was in college during their 1986 season when the Mets made a run for the World Series. I watched almost every game, and those I couldn't watch because I had class at the New York Institute of Technology (NYIT) I would listen to on my portable radio (I know I just dated myself, but that's okay).

The seventh and final game was played on Monday, October 27, 1986, at 8:30 p.m., and I had a night class. I walked into class with my portable radio on and my headphones in. I took the headphones out of my ears because class was about to start, but my professor stopped me and told me that if I was listening to the game I could keep them in. He would give me the notes if I told him if someone scored. That really happened.

The game wasn't over by the time class ended. NYIT is on the corner of 61st and Broadway in New York City. I had a train to catch at Grand Central Station at 42nd Street, but I decided to walk the 20 blocks so I could listen to the game. I peeked in sports bars along the way to watch a batter or two. When I got down to Grand Central Station, the game still wasn't over, but I didn't want to miss my train.

The Mets were winning 8–5, heading into the top of the ninth inning. Three more Boston outs and the championship was ours. As I walked into Grand Central Station, I saw a group of people huddled around a portable television watching the game. I had a few minutes before the train left, so I huddled with them. When the Mets retired the Sox to win the Series, our screams echoed throughout the cavernous train station. It was a moment I have obviously not forgotten. I cried.

There is so much more to sports than just watching it on television. Seeing a game in person and feeling those thunderous chants reverberate in your chest is a feeling like no other. Before I went to NYIT, I spent a semester at Florida State University in Tallahassee and attended two Seminoles football games. So much fun! You have to be at one to truly understand.

Here's my favorite sports story: I am the youngest of four children and I have three older brothers. All of us—including my mom—love sports. My mom watches the Dallas Cowboys every time she can and screams until she's practically hoarse. When I was seven, my father passed away. One of my brothers came up to me and asked who my favorite football team was. I didn't have one at the time, so I asked "who did Daddy root for?" They told me the Green Bay Packers. "I'm a Green Bay Packers fan then," I said.

I had never watched a Packers game and didn't for about two years after I said that. Then I was hooked. I loved football and fell in love with the Green and Gold. Way back then, I decided that one day I was going to go to Green Bay, Wisconsin, and step on the 50 yard line of Lambeau Field. I didn't know how, but I would. I am a die-hard Packers fan and going to Lambeau Field became #2 on my bucket list. While it might seem easy to do, sometimes life takes you in different directions, and you can't exactly take the trips you want to take when you want to take them.

It took me a long time, but on Friday, October 7, 2016, I finally drove up to Lambeau Field, crying as I pulled into the stadium parking lot. On Saturday, October 8, 2016, I took a behind-the-scenes tour of Lambeau, which included walking on the field. My dream came true. There I was on the field! Well, the sidelines—they don't let you step directly on the field, but I had my feet right next to the 50 yard line. I made it! The tour guide even let us stay an extra minute as the others filed out because I told him how this was a bucket list moment for me and I didn't want it to end. I then watched the Packers defeat the New York Giants the next day. I made it to a Packers game at Lambeau. (Side note: My brothers were wrong. My dad was a *Minnesota Vikings* fan! Oh well, I'm not rooting for them now!)

That's the excitement of sports! It's where the idea for this book came from. Sharing my story about Lambeau with others opened up their stories to me. I learned about sports fans who rented vans and went to every professional football stadium or baseball stadium across the country, and fans who even went on cruises with players

---

Travel Tip

Corporate sponsorships change often. Some stadium names may have changed since publication of this book.

Accessible Sports Travel

Candy Harrington is an expert on accessible travel, authoring multiple books on the subject including the *Barrier-Free Travel* series and *101 Accessible Vacations*. She is also the founder of Emerging Horizons, the source for accessible travel news (http://emerginghorizons.com/). So when I was writing this book and thinking about the stadiums and museums being accessible for travelers, I knew I had to talk to her. Here are her tips:

- Don't assume something is not accessible because it's historic. "Take Babe Ruth's birthplace in Maryland, for example. They put an elevator in years ago, so give the place a call or look on the website if you're not sure."
- Most stadiums are accessible. "I haven't encountered a stadium tour that isn't wheelchair accessible. All stadiums are accessible, but the tours may have a different route for a wheelchair to take to see everything, just so you know."
- When it comes to getting accessible tickets to a sporting event, there is typically a separate method. "They don't usually go out into the general population. Mostly professional sports venues have a special number to call to get accessible tickets and they are not more expensive than regular tickets."
- When it comes to big events, like the Super Bowl, Candy says she usually gets questions from fans in January once they know their team has made it. That's a big mistake. "There is a separate lottery for ADA Super Bowl tickets, which takes place from February to September of the previous year. The lottery is drawn in October, so you have to plan ahead for that one. Most people I know who go, do it by venue. For example, if they know the Super Bowl is being played in Atlanta and they know they can get there, they enter. If your name is picked, and you don't want the tickets, you're not obligated, but I really never talked to anyone who has returned them."

from their favorite team. Then I found out about all the sports museums that this country has that many people don't even know about. Add in the locations where some of your favorite sports films were made and all of the sports-related statues—so much to see and do! I wanted to create a one-stop traveling guide to what sports lovers can do in the United States, so I hope you enjoy this book as much as I enjoyed putting it together.

A few notes: I'm sure I missed something, so be sure to contact me and I'll add it to the next edition. For college, I focus mostly on basketball and football and, in many cases, mostly men's basketball, but please support the women too!

And, I have to say it: Go Pack Go!

ALABAMA

Okay, say it with me loud and proud . . . Roll Tide! Baby, we're in Alabama now where your sports life—for the most part—centers around college and the Alabama Crimson Tide sports teams. This is where the legendary Paul "Bear" Bryant was the University of Alabama's head coach for 25 years and won, count 'em, *six* national championships. It's where he motivated his players with such quotes as, "Show class, have pride, and display character. If you do, winning takes care of itself." To honor Bryant's accomplishments and learn more about the impact that he had on this state and his players, make sure to visit Paul W. Bryant Museum in Tuscaloosa, and while you're there, plan your trip during the school's football season so you can also take in a game at Bryant-Denny Stadium. For those of you who want to do a college football tour, it wouldn't be complete without seeing the Auburn University Tigers and the University of Alabama at Birmingham Blazers.

But hang on, because Alabama is more than just football (although you may want to make sure that nobody hears you say that while you're visiting). Alabama is also home to so much baseball history, starting with the fact that two of the biggest legends in the game—Willie Mays and Hank Aaron—were born here. Alabama is also where you will find the oldest baseball stadium in the country, Rickwood Field, and the history of African-American baseball at Birmingham's Negro Southern League Museum.

Speaking of sports history, you can't talk about any of it without mentioning American track-and-field athlete and Olympic superstar Jesse Owens, who was born in Oakville, Alabama. Here, there's a must-see memorial park and museum dedicated to Owens where you can honor the impact that this one man had on the world, especially when he competed at the 1936 Berlin Olympics.

Racing fans should also put Alabama on their vacation list and get here—fast—because this is the home of the famous Talladega Superspeedway, the Barber Vintage Motorsports Museum, and the International Motorsports Hall of Fame.

So much to see, so much to do, so here is your guide to Alabama.

HANK AARON MUSEUM

Baseball legend Hank Aaron was born and raised in Alabama—Mobile to be exact—and briefly appeared in the Negro American League before making his way to the majors. And what a career he had! His accomplishments could fill up page upon page

---

Website: https://www.milb.com/mobile

Info: The Hank Aaron Museum is open Monday through Friday 9 a.m. to 5 p.m. and during the home games of the Mobile BayBears. Cost: adults, $5; children (12 and under), $4. Handicapped accessible.

Contact: Hank Aaron Museum, 755 Bolling Bros. Blvd., Mobile AL 36606; (251) 572-2327.

Reggie Jackson and Hank Aaron at the opening of the Hank Aaron Museum in Mobile, Alabama WIKIMEDIA COMMONS

of this book, but the highlights include more than 3,000 hits and 750 home runs in his career and earning three Gold Gloves for his stellar play in right field.

If you want to see where the legend's career began, check out the Hank Aaron Museum that sits on the property of the Mobile BayBears, who play in the appropriately named Hank Aaron Stadium. This home, which was moved to its current location in 2010 from Toulminville, was originally three rooms built by Hank's dad, but was expanded to seven rooms to help showcase the legend's history in the game.

Statue Alert!

"Say hey Willie, won't you hit one out here! We'll give you a cheer if you do!" There's so much to cheer (or sing) about when it comes to Alabama and baseball. First, this is where the Say Hey Kid, Willie Mays, was born, in Westfield. He played for the Birmingham Black Barons of the Negro American League and went on to play 22 years in Major League Baseball and become one of the biggest names in the history of the game. Mays ended his career with a whopping 660 home runs and earned seven consecutive Gold Gloves. He was elected to Baseball's Hall of Fame in Cooperstown, New York (see page 114) in 1979.

Mays's hometown honors him with a 9 x 8 statue that's located outside the entrance to Regions Field on 14th Street South in Birmingham.

NEGRO SOUTHERN LEAGUE MUSEUM

When they were young, both Hank Aaron and Willie Mays got their baseball starts with the Negro Southern League, which was created in 1920 and lasted for 31 years. The league also included Leroy "Satchel" Paige, Hilton Smith, Norman "Turkey" Stearnes, and George "Mule" Suttles. The league started with eight teams and ended with more than 80 teams participating over three decades. The Negro Southern League Museum, based in Birmingham, pays homage to this league and the players who have left their mark. On your visit, you will see such memorabilia as Satchel Paige's uniform, the McCallister Trophy (the oldest known Negro League trophy), and the Cuban Stars baseball players' contract from 1907 (oldest known contract). You'll also learn about the amazing 1948 Birmingham Black Barons who won the Negro American League championship.

> **Website:** https://www.birminghamnslm.org
>
> **Info:** The Negro Southern League Museum is free to the public and is open Tuesday through Saturday 10 a.m. to 4 p.m. Closed on Sunday and Monday (except on Martin Luther King Day).
>
> **Contact:** Negro Southern League Museum, 120 16th St. South, Birmingham AL 35233; (205) 581-3040.

RICKWOOD FIELD

Named after its founder, Rick Woodward, this Birmingham baseball field is the oldest in the country, opening on August 18, 1910. Woodward connected with Cornelius McGillicuddy, better known as Connie Mack, a professional baseball catcher, manager, and team owner, to help him design the field. The Black Barons from the Negro Southern League played here as did Ty Cobb, Dizzy Dean, and "Shoeless" Joe Jackson.

> **Website:** https://rickwood.com
>
> **Info:** The field is open to visitors and hosts many baseball games and events throughout the year.
>
> **Contact:** Rickwood Field, 1137 2nd Ave. West, Birmingham AL 35204; (205) 999-5742.

TALLADEGA SUPERSPEEDWAY

Gentleman and ladies, start your engines—and then drive to the Talladega Superspeedway, a racetrack every racing fan must see at least once in their life. The Superspeedway started as the Alabama International Motor Speedway in 1989 and has

> **Travel Tip**
>
> Many of the stadiums and venues have their own mobile apps now, so if you're on vacation you can have access to the most up-to-date stadium news and information on your phone or other mobile device.

been the host to some of the best NASCAR racers in history. Check the current calendar for races and, if you've always dreamed of being behind the wheel, why not sign up for a Talladega / Richard Petty and NASCAR Driving Experience while you're there? (For Talladega Superspeedway tours see the International Motorsports Hall of Fame [next].)

Website: www.talladegasuperspeedway.com

Info: Race ticket prices vary. The driving experience packages start at $99.

Contact: Talladega Superspeedway, 3366 Speedway Blvd., Talladega AL 35160; (855) 518-RACE (7223).

INTERNATIONAL MOTORSPORTS HALL OF FAME

This one-hour self-guided tour has three exhibit halls and a library with a whopping 14,000 volumes of books, magazines, and other motorsports research material. The Hall of Fame also offers a 20-minute handicapped accessible tour of the Talladega Superspeedway.

Website: www.motorsportshalloffame.com

Info: The Talladega Superspeedway tours begin at 9 a.m. and run every half hour to 4 p.m. The Hall of Fame is open 9 a.m. to 4 p.m. every day of the year except New Year's, Thanksgiving, Christmas Day, and Easter. Admission to the Hall of Fame: Cost: adults, $12; students (ages 6–12), $5; children 5 and under, free with adult admission. Track tour admission: adults, $8; students (ages 6–12), $5; children 5 and under, free with adult admission. Seniors $1 discount. Museum and speedway tour combo prices: adults, $16; students (ages 6–12), $8; ages 5 and under, free.

Contact: International Motorsports Hall of Fame, 3366 Speedway Blvd., Lincoln AL 35096; (256) 362-5002.

TALLADEGA WALK OF FAME / DAVEY ALLISON MEMORIAL PARK

While you're at the Talladega Superspeedway, take time to honor those who have raced there throughout the years, especially Davey Allison, who was memorialized here after a helicopter crash at Talladega on July 12, 1993, took his life. There is an induction ceremony held the Saturday night of a Talladega race week in September or October.

Website: www.talladegawalk.com

Info: Open 24 hours.

Contact: Talladega Walk of Fame/Davey Allison Memorial Park, Coffee and Court Sts. (behind Police Dept.), Talladega AL 35161; (256) 362-4261.

BARBER VINTAGE MOTORSPORTS MUSEUM

This Birmingham museum is home to a record 1,600 motorcycles spanning over 100 years of production from 20 countries (just ask the *Guinness Book of World Records*!). It was opened by its founder George Barber. Today it also has a 930-acre, 16-turn, 2.38-mile racetrack that is home to the Porsche Sport Driving School. Motorcycle fans will love the Annual Barber Vintage Festival, a three-day festival and swap meet.

Website: https://www.barbermuseum.org

Info: This is very important: check the events calendar before you go. If you attend during an event, you will have to buy both an event ticket and a museum ticket. Cost: adults, $15; children ages 4–12, $10; children 3 and under, free. From April 1 to September 30 the museum is open Monday through Saturday 10 a.m. to 6 p.m. and Sunday noon to 6 p.m. From October 1 to March 31, the museum is open Monday through Saturday 10 a.m. to 5 p.m. and Sunday noon to 5 p.m.

Contact: Barber Vintage Motorsports Museum, 6030 Barber Motorsports Pkwy., Birmingham AL 35094; (205) 699-7275.

ALABAMA SPORTS HALL OF FAME

If you still can't get enough of Alabama's sports history, there are over 5,000 sports artifacts displayed in this 33,000-square-foot building. The museum was created in 1967 and its tagline is "Where heroes live forever." I'm sure you know some of these heroes too, such as baseball's Tommie Agee, boxing's Evander Holyfield, and football's Bobby Bowden.

Website: http://ashof.org

Info: The Alabama Sports Hall of Fame is open Monday through Friday from 9 a.m. to 5 p.m. Cost: adults, $5; senior citizens (ages 60 and older), $4; students, $3; family, $14.

Contact: Alabama Sports Hall of Fame, 2150 Richard Arrington Jr. Blvd. North, Birmingham AL 35203; (205) 323-6665.

JESSE OWENS MEMORIAL PARK

The Jesse Owens Memorial Park honors the Olympic track star with a statue, exhibits, and, of course, a replica of the Olympic torch. While you are here you can go back in time and feel like you're right there at the Olympics with Jesse Owens by watching Bud Greenspan's 1966 film *Return to Berlin*. You can also test your own skills against Owens's at the park's long jump pit and see how close you can come to his 1936 Olympic gold medal distance of 26 feet 5 5⁄16 inches.

Website: http://jesseowensmemorialpark.com/wordpress1/statue

Info: The museum is open Monday through Saturday 10 a.m. to 4 p.m. and Sunday 1 p.m. to 4 p.m. Cost: $5 per person, 4 and under are free.

Contact: Jesse Owens Memorial Park, 7019 County Rd. 203, Danville AL 35619; (256) 974-3636.

COLLEGE SPORTS TOUR

UNIVERSITY OF ALABAMA CRIMSON TIDE / BRYANT-DENNY STADIUM

The University of Alabama's football stadium is named after both Coach "Bear" Bryant and George H. Denny, the school's president from 1912 to 1932. It's the eighth largest stadium in the world. Get tickets to a football game when you're in town and you can watch the current, and also legendary, Crimson Tide football coach Nick Saban at the helm. Since 2007, Saban has led the team to five national championships. Take a behind-the-scenes tour of the stadium where you'll peek into the home team locker room and the recruiting room and walk by the field.

Bryant-Denny Stadium at the University of Alabama WIKIMEDIA COMMONS

Statue Alert

Say cheese! Don't miss the opportunity to take a selfie with Coach Bryant (well, a statue of him) right in front of Bryant-Denny Stadium. A statue of current UA football coach Nick Saban can be found on the Walk of Champions on the UA campus in Tuscaloosa.

PAUL W. BRYANT MUSEUM AND MUSEUM LIBRARY

Don't let the name of this museum fool you. Of course it's about the man—Coach "Bear" Bryant—but it also includes a comprehensive look at the history of Alabama Crimson Tide football, starting back in 1892 and continuing through the present day. The exhibits include the Hall of Honor and a peek into Coach's "office" where you can just imagine the inspirational talks he had with his players. The museum underwent renovations in 2019 and added an interactive video wall where visitors can access team databases.

AUBURN UNIVERSITY TIGERS / JORDAN-HARE STADIUM

The Auburn University Tigers football team plays at Jordan-Hare Stadium. According to the stadium's history, it is named after Ralph "Shug" Jordan, Auburn's all-time winningest football coach, and Clifford Leroy Hare, a member of Auburn's first football team, president of the old Southern Conference, and longtime chairman of Auburn's Faculty Athletic Committee. Auburn officially began competing in intercollegiate football in 1892 and won their first national championship in 1913. In 2010, quarterback Cam Newton, who spent just one year at Auburn, led the Tigers to their first national championship since 1957 and became the third Auburn player to win the Heisman Trophy. Newton now plays for the NFL's Carolina Panthers.

Website: https://auburntigers.com

Info: There are locker room tours on Fridays before home games. The lower level of the stadium where the locker rooms are is handicapped accessible, but the tour may include other parts of the stadium that are not accessible.

Contact: Jordan-Hare Stadium, 251 S Donahue Dr., Auburn AL 36849; (334) 844-4750.

SENIOR BOWL / MOBILE ALABAMA BOWL / LADD-PEEBLES STADIUM

Every January, the Reese's Senior Bowl is played the weekend prior to the Super Bowl in Mobile, at Ladd-Peebles Stadium. The Senior Bowl features the country's best senior collegiate football players and top NFL draft prospects on teams representing the North and South. The teams are coached by the coaching staffs of two NFL teams. So you could be seeing future NFL players if you're lucky enough to get a ticket to the game.

At the Senior Bowl Museum, you will learn how the first Senior Bowl game was played in 1950, and much more through touch-screen displays, video clips, and photos. Can you guess which NFL legends once participated in the Senior Bowl? Here's one spoiler—former Green Bay Packers quarterback Brett Favre—but to learn the rest you really should visit!

Website: https://www.seniorbowl.com and https://lmobilealabamabowl.com

Info: Tickets to the bowl games can be purchased through their websites. The Senior Bowl Museum is open to the public Monday through Friday 9 a.m. to 4 p.m. and is free. Handicapped accessible.

Contacts: Senior Bowl Museum, 151 Dauphin St., Mobile AL 36604; (251) 438-2276. Ladd-Peebles Stadium, 1621 Virginia St., Mobile AL 36604; (251) 208-2500.

Statue Alert!

There's a statue honoring former Auburn quarterback Cam Newton outside Jordan-Hare Stadium.

Good Eats

Looking for something good to eat while you're traveling? Sports fans will love Baumhower's Victory Grille. Why? It's owned by former Crimson Tide and Miami Dolphins defensive lineman Bob Baumhower. Today, Baumhower's has 10 Alabama locations and serves typical game day fare, such as football, wings, and beer. For more information and a complete menu, visit https://baumhowers.com.

The Mobile Alabama Bowl (also played at Ladd-Peebles Stadium) pits a team from the Sun Belt Conference against one from the Mid-American Conference.

UNIVERSITY OF ALABAMA AT BIRMINGHAM BLAZERS / BARTOW ARENA

The University of Alabama at Birmingham Blazers basketball team play at the Bartow Arena.

Website: https://uabsports.com

Info: No "official" behind-the-scenes stadium tours, but I was told that there is no cost to enter and walk around.

Contact: Bartow Arena, East Tower, 617 13th St. South, Birmingham AL 35294; (205) 975-8221.

ALASKA

Alaska is the largest state in the country, but just because it's the biggest doesn't mean it has room for any professional sports teams. But what Alaska does have is the Iditarod, an annual competitive dog sledding race that takes place for 1,150 miles from Anchorage to Nome. The Iditarod started in 1973 and every March "mushers" from around the world come to Alaska with their teams of 16 dogs and race for up to 15 days.

Website: https://iditarod.com

Contact: Iditarod Trail Committee, 2100 S Knik Goose Bay Rd., Wasilla AK 99687; (800) 545-6874.

Travel Tip

If you are traveling with a group, always ask in advance about rates. I have listed group rates for certain attractions, but they may be available even if they aren't noted here.

ARIZONA

It's known as the Grand Canyon State for obvious reasons (it's home to the beautiful and majestic Grand Canyon, in case you didn't know), but there are so many other reasons to book your trip here. Arizona will host another Super Bowl in 2023 as well as the NCAA Men's Final Four Championship in 2024. When it comes to Major League Baseball, the Arizona Diamondbacks are exciting to watch, and basketball fans will love rooting on the NBA's Phoenix Suns.

Your college sports tour should include stops to watch the University of Arizona Wildcats, the Arizona Sun Devils, and the Northern Arizona Lumberjacks. Arizona sports isn't done yet—you have professional football, hockey, and even an indoor football team. Racing fans can gather at the ISM Raceway for NASCAR events.

ARIZONA DIAMONDBACKS / CHASE FIELD

Take me out to the ballgame—and make it a D-backs game! The Arizona Diamondbacks entered Major League Baseball as an expansion team in 1998 and won their first, and so far only, World Series championship in 2001 against the New York Yankees. They play their games at Chase Field in Phoenix, which offers a 75-minute behind-the-scenes walking tour. Unfortunately,

Website: https://www.mlb.com/dbacks

Info: Chase Field tours are offered Monday through Saturday at 9:30 a.m., 11 a.m., and 12:30 p.m. Cost: adults, $7; children (ages 4–6), $3; seniors, $5; children ages 3 and under, free. There are no tours on Sundays. Visit the website for group tour prices and game day ticket prices.

Contact: Chase Field, 401 E Jefferson St., Phoenix AZ 85004; (602) 462-6799.

Chase Field, home of the Arizona Diamondbacks
WIKIMEDIA COMMONS, PHOTO BY MELENIE OTTOSEN

you won't get to walk on the field, but touring this incredible venue is definitely worth the price of the ticket.

By the way, don't worry about overheating while watching a Diamondbacks game because of that so-called dry heat that Arizona residents talk about. The retractable roof keeps fans cool during the summer months.

CACTUS LEAGUE EXPERIENCE

Spring training and Arizona go hand in hand. The Cactus League Experience shows visitors the 100-year history of MLB spring training in Arizona. You'll learn where it all started and hear about the formation of the Cactus League in 1947. Learn how some of the greats were once here including Ty Cobb, Willie Mays (who homered at Phoenix Municipal Stadium), Mickey Mantle, and Joe DiMaggio. There are uniforms, programs, and autographed items. There's so much to do, watch, and listen to here, including film montages and announcers calling the game.

Website: https://www.azspringtrainingexperience.com

Contact: Cactus League Experience, Tempe Diablo Stadium, 2200 W Alameda Dr., Tempe AZ 85282; (480) 835-2286.

It's downright hot in Arizona, but it's super cool to visit the Cactus League Experience at the Tempe Diablo Stadium. ARIZONA OFFICE OF TOURISM

Sports Film Fact

Show me the money! *Jerry Maguire* was one of Tom Cruise's most popular movies. In this 1996 blockbuster film, Cruise plays a sports agent who, after getting fired, starts his own management company. He starts by trying to sign sought-after football player Rod Tidwell, played by Cuba Gooding Jr. Scenes in the movie were filmed around Arizona, including at Flat Iron Peak in the Superstition Mountains of Lost Dutchman State Park, 40 miles east of Phoenix. The football game where Tidwell gets knocked out was played and filmed in Sun Devil Stadium.

PHOENIX SUNS / TALKING STICK RESORT ARENA

If b-ball is your thing, then take in a Phoenix Suns game at the Talking Stick Resort Arena in Phoenix. This NBA expansion team hasn't won a championship—yet—but its history includes such legends as Charles Barkley, Paul Westphal, Amar'e Stoudemire, and Steve Nash.

Website: www.talkingstickresortarena.com

Contact: Talking Stick Resort Arena, 201 East Jefferson St., Phoenix AZ 85004; (602) 379-7800.

ARIZONA CARDINALS / STATE FARM STADIUM

The oldest pro football team in continuous existence in the United States, the Cardinals date back more than 100 years to 1898. In their record-setting history, they have won two championships—1925 and 1947. Get tickets to see them play and, while you're there, take a 90-minute walking tour of their State Farm Stadium, where college football's Fiesta Bowl is also played (check out the Ziegler Fiesta Bowl Museum below). Here you will have the opportunity to see the press box, tour the visiting team's locker room, check out a private loft, and step on the stadium field.

Website: https://www.azcardinals.com and https://fiestabowl.org/fiesta-bowl

Info: The stadium tour is ADA accessible and wheelchairs are also available. Tours are not offered on Arizona Cardinals game days, but you can take a tour Wednesday through Saturday at 10:30 a.m., 12:30 p.m., or 2:30 p.m. Cost: adult, $9; juniors (4–12), $7; seniors, $7; military, $7; children ages 3 and younger, free.

Contact: State Farm Stadium, 1 Cardinals Dr., Glendale AZ 85305; (623) 433-7101.

Statue Alert!

Pat Tillman played linebacker for the Arizona State University Sun Devils and then was drafted by the Arizona Cardinals. After the devastating September 11th attacks, he left the NFL and joined the US Army. He served in both Iraq and Afghanistan and died on April 22, 2004, at age 27 from friendly fire. Tillman is honored with a statue at ASU's Sun Devil Stadium that was placed right outside the players' tunnel.

ZIEGLER FIESTA BOWL MUSEUM

Whether or not you got a ticket to the Fiesta Bowl game, you should still visit the Ziegler Fiesta Bowl Museum and browse the memorabilia from previous bowl games. There are Heisman awards and other trophies for you to see.

Website: https://fiestabowl.org/ziegler-fiesta-bowl-museum

Info: The museum is free. It is open Monday through Friday 8:30 a.m. to 5 p.m.

Contact: Ziegler Fiesta Bowl Museum, 7135 E. Camelback Rd., Suite 190, Scottsdale AZ 85251; (480) 350-0900.

ARIZONA RATTLERS / TALKING STICK RESORT ARENA

Can't get enough of the pigskin? Then check out the Arizona Rattlers, an Indoor Football League team that was founded in 1992 and plays at the Talking Stick Resort Arena. The IFL plays a 17-week season that runs from February through June. It was started back in 2003 as the Intense Football League.

Website: www.azrattlers.com

Info: For a complete list of IFL teams, visit http://goifl.com/members.

Contact: 201 E. Jefferson St., Phoenix AZ 85004; (602) 514-TDTD (8383).

ARIZONA COYOTES / GILA RIVER ARENA

Originally known as the Phoenix Coyotes, this NHL team was once coached by the legendary Wayne Gretzky, from 2005 to 2009. Although they do not have any championships yet, you can still take in a game at the Gila River Arena in Glendale.

Website: https://www.nhl.com/coyotes and www.gilariverarena.com

Contact: Arizona Coyotes, 9400 West Maryland Ave., Glendale AZ 85305; (623) 772-3200.

ISM RACEWAY

NASCAR fans will love watching the races at the ISM Raceway, formerly called the Phoenix International Raceway. It was built in 1964 with the hope that it would become the "Indianapolis of the West" and includes a one-mile oval, a quarter-mile drag strip, and a 2.5-mile road course. Racing legends Kurt Busch, Jeff Gordon, Ricky Rudd, Jimmy Johnson, and Cale Yarborough have raced here, and even actor Steve McQueen once raced on this track in 1970.

Website: https://www.ismraceway.com

Info: Check out the racing schedule before planning your visit.

Contact: ISM Raceway, 125 S. Avondale Blvd., Suite 200, Avondale AZ 85323; (866) 408-RACE (7223).

The ISM Raceway in Avondale hosts many NASCAR races.
ARIZONA OFFICE OF TOURISM

PENSKE RACING MUSEUM

Less than a half-hour away from the ISM Raceway is the Penske Racing Museum, which is a mecca of Penske's 50 years of racing memorabilia, including cars and trophies. The Penske Racing Team has had 440 major race wins and 16 Indianapolis 500 victories to date. Here you will see replicas of their winning cars, such as the 1963 Pontiac Catalina that Roger Penske drove in the 1963 NASCAR Riverside 250 and the Dallara that Hélio Castroneves used to win the 2009 Indianapolis 500.

Website: https://www.penskeautomall.com/museum

Info: The museum is open Monday through Saturday 8 a.m. to 4 p.m. and Sunday noon to 5 p.m. Handicapped accessible.

Contact: Penske Racing Museum, 7125 E. Chauncey Ln., Phoenix AZ 85054; (480) 538-4444.

COLLEGE SPORTS TOUR

The biggest college sports rivalry in Arizona is between the University of Arizona Wildcats and Arizona State University's Sun Devils. They compete once a year in a "Duel for the Desert" where teams fight for bragging rights and the Territorial Cup. The game alternates between Tucson and Tempe.

UNIVERSITY OF ARIZONA WILDCATS / ARIZONA STADIUM

Bear down! Located in Tucson, the University of Arizona's teams are members of the Pac-12 Conference of the NCAA. You'll definitely want to take in a football or basketball game while you're there. You should also visit their Jim Click Hall of Champions, which is a nearly 10,000-square-foot venue that displays over 100 years of the university's sports history.

Website: https://arizonawildcats.com

Info: Handicapped accessible. Most of the year the Jim Click Hall of Champions hours are Monday through Friday 8 a.m. to 5 p.m. and Saturday 9 a.m. to 1 p.m. (closed Sunday). Summer hours are Monday through Friday 8 a.m. to 3 p.m. (closed Saturday and Sunday). Also typically closed on Saturday in late December and early January—call ahead for exact dates.

Contact: Arizona Stadium, 545 N National Championship Dr., Tucson AZ 85719; (520) 621-2211.

ARIZONA STATE SUN DEVILS / SUN DEVIL STADIUM

The Pac-10's Arizona State Sun Devils have won 17 conference titles (as of this printing) and play in Sun Devil Stadium, the only stadium that is located between two mountains. The stadium hosted the 1996 Super Bowl.

Website: https://thesundevils.com

Contact: Sun Devil Stadium, 500 E Veterans Way, Tempe AZ 85287; (480) 727-0000.

NORTHERN ARIZONA LUMBERJACKS / WALKUP SKYDOME

While the college sports talk in Arizona centers around the Sun Devils and the Wildcats, don't forget about Northern Arizona University, located in Flagstaff. Home to the Lumberjacks, they are a member of the Big Sky Conference and sponsor 15 NCAA Division I level athletic programs.

Website: https://nauathletics.com

Contact: Northern Arizona University, 1705 South San Francisco St., Flagstaff AZ 86011; (928) 523-5353.

Good Eats

What do you do when you're done playing professional basketball? You open up a restaurant—or five. In 1992, former Phoenix Suns guard/forward "Thunder Dan" Majerle opened up his first restaurant, Majerle's Sports Grill, and now has five locations throughout Arizona—in Scottsdale, Phoenix, Flagstaff, Desert Ridge, and Goodyear. Majerle played eight seasons in Phoenix (1988–1995 and 2001–02). At his restaurants, you can enjoy such noshes as "Slam Dunk" Shrimp and Gorilla Wings.
WEBSITE: http://majerles.com

This Pat Tillman statue can be found at Arizona State University's Sun Devil Stadium.
WIKIMEDIA COMMONS

ARKANSAS

This state borders the Mississippi River and is known for its luscious wilderness and being the only location in the United States where you can mine for your own diamonds—but let's focus on that sports history! Many notable coaches and athletes were born here, including Paul "Bear" Bryant, baseball's great Lou Brock, PGA star John Daly, New York Yankees catcher Bill Dickey, and Green Bay Packers defensive tackle Dave "Hawg" Hanner. College sports fans must check out the excitement of a Razorbacks game too. You can learn more about Arkansas sports history at their Hall of Fame in North Little Rock.

ARKANSAS SPORTS HALL OF FAME

Arkansas makes sure to pay respects to the teams and individuals who make Arkansas sports special. At the Arkansas Sports Hall of Fame, you'll find exhibits on football, a tribute to sports trainers, and memorabilia like seats from former stadiums, as well as track and field exhibits.

Website: https://www.arksportshalloffame.com

Info: The museum is open by appointment only so make sure you call ahead. Cost: adults (ages 18-61), $6; seniors (ages 62 and older), $4; children (ages 6-17), $3; active military with proper identification, $3; children 6 and under, free.

Contact: Arkansas Sports Hall of Fame, #3 Verizon Arena Way, North Little Rock AR 72114; (501) 313-4158.

MARK MARTIN EXHIBIT

Former NASCAR driver Mark Martin set up an exhibit that is dedicated to, well, him, and it's inside his Batesville Ford dealership. On display: his championship cars, suits, helmets, and trophies. Mark Martin's Hall of Fame career spanned 32 years and four decades, from 1981 to 2013. In that time, he won the 1989 Richard Petty Driver of the Year award and became the IROC Champion five times with the most wins in IROC history. He is widely considered the greatest driver in racing history to never win a NASCAR Cup.

Info: The dealership is open Monday through Friday 8 a.m. to 6 p.m., Saturday 9 a.m. to 5 p.m. Admission is free.

Contact: Mark Martin Ford Mercury, 1601 Batesville Blvd., Batesville AR; (870) 793-4461.

COLLEGE SPORTS TOUR

University of Arkansas Razorbacks / Donald W. Reynolds Razorback Stadium

Can you believe that the first season of Razorback football was way back in 1894? There have been many coaches throughout those years, naturally, but none as memorable as Lou Holtz, who served as head football coach from 1977 through 1983. Holtz went on to coach at Notre Dame and has a statue dedicated to him outside of the stadium. The Razorbacks claimed the 1964 national championship. They play at the Donald W. Reynolds Razorback Stadium in Fayetteville, and if you're going to see a game, you should know one thing—"Woooooooo. Pig. Sooie! Woooooooo. Pig. Sooie! Woooooooo. Pig. Sooie! Razorbacks!"

Website: https://arkansasrazorbacks.com

Contact: Donald W. Reynolds Razorback Stadium, 350 N Razorback Rd., Fayetteville AR 72701; (479) 575-6533.

University of Arkansas Razorbacks Basketball / Bud Walton Arena

The Razorbacks basketball team played at Bud Walton Arena for the first time in November 1993. That debut year they went 31-3 for the season and won the 1994 national championship! Before the game starts, make sure you tour the museum, located on the ground level, that pays homage to the Razorbacks sports teams, including the championship team and their track and field, baseball, tennis, and golf teams.

Website: https://arkansasrazorbacks.com/facility/bud-walton-arena

Contact: Bud Walton Arena, 1270 Leroy Pond Dr., Fayetteville AR 72701; (479) 575-5151.

CALIFORNIA

Sit back, sports fans, because California has a whopping 19 professional sports teams as well as numerous college sports teams to check off on your sports travel tours. There are also multiple sports museums as well as things to do for fans of NASCAR, golf, and the beautiful game of *futbol* (soccer to us). You will need an extended California stay or multiple trips to see everything.

LOS ANGELES ANGELS / ANGEL STADIUM PARK

This American League team has a storied history that began with—believe it or not—the legendary actor, singer, and rodeo performer Gene Autry. Back in 1961, the "Singing Cowboy" bought the rights to the franchise name for $350,000 and held onto the team for 36 years, but it never won a championship. Later, the Walt Disney Company took control of the team. They won the World Series in 2002. Another change in ownership took place in 2003, when Arturo Moreno bought the team.

If you want to get an up-close look at Angel Stadium, take their 75-minute walking tour where you can see the field, walk through the dugout, and check out the broadcast booth.

Website: https://www.mlb.com/angels/ballpark/tours

Info: The tours run from March to September and private tours are offered in January and February. Cost: adults, $8; children (ages 3-14), $6; seniors (ages 55 and older), and military, $6; children ages 3 and under, free.

Contact: Angel Stadium of Anaheim, 2000 Gene Autry Way, Anaheim CA 92806; (714) 940-2230.

Did you know? The Angels play a part in many Hollywood movies. Let's start with the remake of the 1951 film *Angels in the Outfield* (1994). The team is also featured in *The Naked Gun* (1988), *Taking Care of Business* (1991), *Talent for the Game* (1991), *Air Bud: Seventh Inning Fetch* (2002), and *Deuce Bigalow: Male Gigolo* (1999).

LOS ANGELES DODGERS / DODGER STADIUM

They started as the Brooklyn Grays back in 1883, but became the Los Angeles Dodgers in 1958 and have captured the World Series title five times since. Such legendary baseball players as Sandy Koufax, Orel Hershiser, Dusty Baker, Steve Garvey, Ron Cey, Fernando Valenzuela, and of course Jackie Robinson—the first African American to play Major League Baseball—have worn the Dodgers uniform over the years.

To learn more about the stadium, its famous players, and the Dodgers team history, take their 90-minute walking tour, which includes checking out the field, a close-up view of the dugout, and the World Series trophies. They also offer a separate clubhouse tour that you can see along with the regular Dodger Stadium tour. You'll get a look at the Dodger bullpen, weight room, batting cage, clubhouse, and interview room. Dodger Stadium also offers different pop-up tours, including one on #42, Jackie Robinson—so check the website for their most recent schedules.

Website: https://www.mlb.com/dodgers

Info: Regular Dodger Stadium tours are given at 10 a.m., 11:30 a.m., and 1 p.m. Cost: adults, $20; children (ages 4–14), seniors (ages 55 and older), and military personnel, $15; children ages 3 and under do not require tickets. Handicapped accessible. The two-hour Clubhouse Tour runs on some Saturdays–Sundays–check the website for the complete schedule.

Contact: Dodger Stadium, 1000 Vin Scully Ave., Los Angeles CA 90012; (866) DODGERS.

Did you know? There's a Jackie Robinson museum in New York. There's more information in the New York section or you can visit www.jackierobinson.org.

OAKLAND ATHLETICS / OAKLAND–ALAMEDA COUNTY COLISEUM

They landed in Oakland, but the A's history goes way back to Philadelphia in 1901 when the franchise began. They have won four World Series titles while in Oakland with such legendary players as shortstop Bert Campaneris; outfielders Rickey Henderson, José Canseco, and Reggie Jackson; starting pitchers Jim "Catfish" Hunter and Vida Blue; and relief pitchers Rollie Fingers and Dennis Eckersley. In 2018, the A's announced that they are building a new stadium at Howard Terminal on the waterfront, which will open in 2023.

Websites: https://www.mlb.com/athletics and www.coliseum.com

Info: Oracle Arena–former home of the NBA's Golden State Warriors–is right next to the Oakland–Alameda County Coliseum, so you can combine tours if you prefer. If you do, the double-venue tour will last 2.5 hours with a 15-minute break in between. Tours book 30 days in advance. Tour the Oakland–Alameda County Coliseum for $20, the Oracle Arena for $30, or dual-venue tours for $33.

Contact: Oakland–Alameda County Coliseum, 7000 Coliseum Way, Oakland CA 94621; (510) 569-2121.

SAN DIEGO PADRES / PETCO PARK

The San Diego Padres haven't won a World Series championship yet, but if you love baseball you should still take in a game and send them some good mojo while you're there. You never know when it will be their year to get their rings. Make sure you take a behind-the-scenes tour of the Padres' Petco Park, which will put you right in the press box, the dugout, and the visitors' clubhouse. Handicapped accessible.

Website: https://www.mlb.com/padres and https://www.mlb.com/padres/ballpark/tours

Info: Check the Petco Park website for dates that the tours are not available. Cost: adults, $20; seniors (ages 60 and older), children (ages 12 and under), and military, $17; children under 36 inches tall, free.

Contact: Petco Park, 100 Park Blvd., San Diego CA 92101; (619) 795-5555.

Did you know? McDonald's founder Ray Kroc owned the San Diego Padres from 1974 until his death in 1984.

SAN FRANCISCO GIANTS / ORACLE PARK

It's a baseball team whose history dates back to the late 1800s and starts in New York. Have you ever heard of "The Shot Heard 'Round the World?" It happened in 1951 when the New York Giants' Bobby Thomson hit a game-winning home run off Brooklyn Dodgers pitcher Ralph Branca to win the National League pennant. *"The Giants win the pennant! The Giants win the pennant!"* The New York Giants moved to San Francisco in 1957 and have won a total of eight World Series championships.

And, of course, we can't talk about the Giants without talking about the Say Hey Kid, Willie Mays, and "The Catch." Who knows how he did it, but Mays made a spectacular play in the first game of the 1954 World Series. With his back to the batter, Mays caught a potentially game-winning hit without even looking back. Unbelievable.

Oracle Park offers don't-miss tours of the stadium. You will be able to step foot on the field, sit in the dugout, see the visitors' clubhouse, and enjoy the Giant Vault, a new San Francisco Giants museum. Every season the museum's exhibits will change, which gives you a perfect reason to go back to the stadium again and again.

Website: https://www.mlb.com/giants and https://www.mlb.com/giants/ballpark

Info: Check the website for each season's blackout dates for tours. Cost: adults, $22; seniors (ages 55 and older), $17; children (12 and under), $12; active military (w/valid ID) and 2 and under, free.

Contact: Oracle Park, 24 Willie Mays Plaza, San Francisco CA 94107; (415) 972-2000.

Statue Alert!
A statue of the Say Hey Kid, Willie Mays, greets you at Oracle Park, so get your cameras ready before you go in to watch a game.

A Fan's San Francisco Giants Spring Training Story—Kathy Sena

We live in Los Angeles, but we are San Francisco Giants fans, due to my husband growing up in Monterey and going to Giants games at Candlestick when he was a boy. Plus, what woman doesn't enjoy gazing upon Brandon Crawford and Buster Posey?!

So we hold down the fort for the Giants here in Los Angeles. It's a six-hour drive from Los Angeles to Scottsdale to see the team during spring training and sometimes that's easier and less expensive than planning a trip to San Francisco. We get a package through the Giants vacation planning services that includes hotel, game tickets, one-day early admission, and a BBQ with some of the players. (Other teams do similar packages. Check your team's website for a link.)

The word *spring* can be misleading though. It can be hot in March in Arizona and Florida. Once, when we went to Scottsdale to see the Giants, the city tied its high-temperature record for that date, so bring water. Most ballparks will let you bring it in for spring training if it's sealed. Check your team's website first.

Here are some other tips:

- Check ahead of time to see if your seats are in the shade. If not, bring a hand towel from your hotel, wet it, and wear it under your hat to help keep you cool and keep the sun off your neck. (Yes. Very sexy.)
- If you're sitting on the outfield grass, arrive early to find a spot under a tree if possible.
- Bring sunscreen.
- Take advantage of any early-admission opportunities, either through the ballpark or through any spring training travel package you buy. It's fun to see batting practice and workouts up close, and often the players are happy to sign balls for the kids.

I love the intimacy of the ballpark at spring training. Scottsdale Stadium holds around 10,000 people when it's packed, and there really aren't any bad seats (except for that nasty sun issue). The crowd is generally older, with a lot of retirees, and it's a relaxed atmosphere. The people who come to spring training are true fans and really know the game. We aren't retired, but we make it a point to take time off work to head to Scottsdale every spring to take in a few games.

JOE DIMAGGIO PLAYGROUND

Joltin' Joe DiMaggio played his entire major league career with the New York Yankees, but as a child he and his siblings played in this community park in San Francisco that was later named after him. The playground has a swimming pool; a library; a clubroom; tennis, basketball, and bocce courts; and a children's playground. There's a plaque dedicated to DiMaggio, and you can walk around the park while you're visiting the area like he did as a child.

> **Website:** http://dimaggioplayground.org
>
> **Contact:** DiMaggio Playground, 651 Lombard St., San Francisco CA 94133.

COLLEGE SPORTS TOUR

UNIVERSITY OF SOUTHERN CALIFORNIA (USC) TROJANS / LOS ANGELES MEMORIAL COLISEUM

Fight on! The USC Trojans have won seven out of their last 10 bowl games, making them an exciting team to watch, so don't miss a game while you're in the area. They play at the Los Angeles Memorial Coliseum, which has also been home to the first Super Bowl in 1967 and two Summer Olympic Games (1932 and 1984). There's a Memorial Court of Honor, an area of plaques commemorating people and events that have played a part in the Coliseum's history.

> **Website:** https://usctrojans.com and https://www.lacoliseum.com
>
> **Info:** During the writing of this book, the Coliseum was undergoing construction and there was no end date in sight, so there weren't any tours. Call the Coliseum or visit their website for up-to-date tour information.
>
> **Contact:** Los Angeles Memorial Coliseum, 3911 S Figueroa St., Los Angeles CA 90037; (213) 747-7111.

UCLA BRUINS / ROSE BOWL

If you're trying to see all the college sports stadiums, the Rose Bowl should be at the top of your list. Home to the UCLA Bruins, it celebrates its centennial in 2022 and has been used for more than just football through the years, including the 1932 and 1984 Olympic Games, five Super Bowls, the 1994 World Cup, and the 1999 Women's World Cup. But it's really about football here and, of course, the Rose Bowl parade!

And I know we're talking football, but when you are talking UCLA sports, you have to mention the "Wizard of Westwood," John Wooden, who won 10 NCAA national championships—seven of them in a row—in a 12-year period as head coach.

> **Website:** https://uclabruins.com
>
> **Info:** Tours of the Rose Bowl are held on the last Friday of every month at 10:30 a.m. and 12:30 p.m. You'll visit the original 1922 Locker Room and the field. Cost: adults, $17.50; seniors and children (5-12), $14.50.
>
> **Contact:** Rose Bowl, 1001 Rose Bowl Dr., Pasadena CA 91103; (626) 585-6800.

UCLA ATHLETICS HALL OF FAME

Want to learn more about the Rose Bowl, UCLA, and Coach Wooden? Then check out the UCLA Athletics Hall of Fame, located on the campus at the J. D. Morgan Center. Here you can see a Heisman Trophy, Wooden Awards, and other Wooden memorabilia, video highlights, and so much more. You'll see a complete history of the Bruins from the early 1900s to the present.

Website: https://uclabruins.com/sports/2013/4/17/208274086.aspx

Info: The Hall of Fame is open weekdays from 8 a.m. to 5 p.m. It's closed on most weekends, but is open the first Saturday of every month from 10 a.m. to 4 p.m. Closed for university holidays. Free admission.

Contact: UCLA Athletics Hall of Fame, 325 Westwood Plaza, Los Angeles CA 90095; (310) 825-8699.

ROSE BOWL PARADE

The first Tournament of Roses Parade took place in 1890 and has become an annual New Year's Day pregame tradition ever since. The two-hour event includes beautiful larger-than-life floats and entertainment, and is a must-see if you're in the area.

Website: https://tournamentofroses.com

Info: There are a variety of Rose Bowl Parade ticket packages. Visit the Rose Bowl Parade website for more information.

Contact: Rose Bowl, 1001 Rose Bowl Dr., Pasadena CA 91103; (626) 585-6800.

Are you ready for some NFL football? Because California has *three* professional football teams—the Los Angeles Chargers, the Los Angeles Rams, and the San Francisco 49ers. Yes, there once was the Oakland Raiders too, but they were scheduled to leave for Las Vegas by the time this book came out, so we moved them to the Nevada section.

As of the writing of this book, there are other stadium changes. The Los Angeles Chargers played their home games at Dignity Health Sports Park and the Los Angeles Rams played at LA Memorial Coliseum, but as of the 2020 football season, they will share the newly constructed Los Angeles Stadium at Hollywood Park. Visit the teams' websites for up-to-date information on tickets and stadium tours.

Websites: https://www.chargers.com and https://www.therams.com

SAN FRANCISCO 49ERS / LEVI'S STADIUM / 49ERS MUSEUM

The name "49ers" comes from the prospectors who arrived in Northern California during the 1849 Gold Rush. The San Francisco 49ers, who have won five Super Bowls—all of them between 1981 and 1995— play their games at Levi's Stadium.

In addition to taking in a 49ers game and stadium tour, there is also a museum where you can learn about the history of the team.

Website: www.nfl.com/teams/sanfrancisco49ers and www.levisstadium.com

Info: The 49ers museum is open Friday through Sunday 10 a.m. to 4 p.m. Cost: adults, $15; children (ages 5–12), Santa Clara residents, seniors, and military, $10; children 4 and under, free.

Contact: Levi's Stadium (and museum), 4900 Marie P. DeBartolo Way, Santa Clara CA 95054; (408) 673-2100.

STAPLES CENTER

The Staples Center in Los Angeles is home to the NBA's Los Angeles Lakers and Los Angeles Clippers, as well as the Los Angeles Sparks of the Women's National Basketball Association and the Los Angeles Kings of the National Hockey League.

Contact: Staples Center, 1111 S. Figueroa St., Los Angeles CA 90015; (213) 742-7100.

LOS ANGELES LAKERS

Shaquille O'Neal, Kobe Bryant, Magic Johnson, Jerry West, Wilt Chamberlain, and Kareem Abdul-Jabbar are just a few of the legendary Lakers who have made the game so exciting over the years and given the team 16 NBA championships.

Website: https://www.nba.com/lakers

LOS ANGELES CLIPPERS

Blake Griffin and Chris Paul are just two of the most famous Los Angeles Clippers through the franchise's history that began back in 1970. The team was once the Buffalo Braves and featured the incredible forward Bob McAdoo. Unfortunately the franchise has yet to win a championship.

Website: https://www.nba.com/clippers

LOS ANGELES KINGS

The Kings have won two Stanley Cups since they were founded back in June 1967. They were one of the six teams that became part of the 1967 NHL expansion.

Website: https://www.nhl.com/kings

Did you know? The Los Angeles Kings legend Wayne Gretzky (who played for the team from 1988 to 1996) is also honored at Canada's Alberta Sports Hall of Fame and Museum? Visit https://ashfm.ca for more information.

GOLDEN STATE WARRIORS / ORACLE ARENA

They started in Philly, but this NBA team made their way to the West Coast back in 1962. They've won six NBA championships, including in 1975 when they defeated the heavily favored Baltimore Bullets in a four-game sweep, and three titles in recent years with help from such superstars as Kevin Durant and Stephen Curry. The team formerly played their games at the Oracle Arena, but will be moving to the Chase Center in San Francisco for the 2019-20 season.

Websites: https://www.nba.com/teams/warriors and www.chasecenter.com

Info: The Chase Center will open in 2020. Call ahead for information on tours.

Contact: Chase Center, 1 Warriors Way, San Francisco CA 94158; (888) GSW-HOOP.

SACRAMENTO KINGS / GOLDEN 1 CENTER

The Kings were founded in 1923 and have only one NBA championship, earned back in 1951 when they were known as the Rochester Royals. Many great players have tried for a repeat, including Metta World Peace (formerly known as Ron Artest), Mitch Richmond, Brad Miller, Mike Bibby, and Chris Webber.

Website: https://www.nba.com/kings; https://www.golden1center.com

Contact: Golden 1 Center, 500 David J. Stern Walk, Sacramento CA 95814; (888) 91-KINGS.

ANAHEIM DUCKS / HONDA CENTER

The Anaheim Ducks are named after the Mighty Ducks from the Walt Disney movie of the same name. In addition to their Stanley Cup win in 2007, the Ducks have made the playoffs 14 times and won six Pacific Division titles (2006-07, 2012-13, 2013-14, 2014-15, 2015-16, and 2016-17) and two Western Conference championships (2002-03 and 2006-07). The Honda Center arena is also home to the NCAA Big West Basketball Tournament.

Website: https://www.nhl.com/ducks and https://www.hondacenter.com

Contact: Honda Center, 2695 E Katella Ave., Anaheim CA 92806; (714) 704-2400.

SAN JOSE SHARKS / SAP CENTER

Go Sharks! The San Jose Sharks are an NHL franchise that started playing in the 1991-92 season. They play at the SAP Center, now known informally as the "Shark Tank." Unfortunately, the Stanley Cup trophy has been out of their reach, although they have made it to the finals once so far.

Website: https://www.nhl.com/sharks and www.sapcenter.com

Contact: SAP Center, 525 W Santa Clara St., San Jose CA 95113; (408) 287-7070.

LA GALAXY / DIGNITY HEALTH SPORTS PARK

The winningest team in Major League Soccer (MLS), the LA Galaxy, has five MLS Cup titles since the league started in 1996. In 2007, one of the most famous athletes ever, English player David Beckham, was brought over from England to play for the Galaxy, and he stayed for five years. The Galaxy play their games at Dignity Health Sports Park, which has been the venue for the 2003 MLS All-Star Game, the MLS Cup (2003, 2004, 2008, 2011, 2012, 2014) and various US National team soccer matches. A stadium like this deserves a tour, where you can walk where the players walk, see the trophy case, and look at the players' weight room.

Website: https://www.lagalaxy.com

Info: Tours of Dignity Health Sports Park are offered Tuesday through Friday. Tours start at 2 p.m. Reservations must be made 48 hours in advance to confirm availability. Groups of 35 members or less: adults, $12; children under 18, $7. Groups of 35 members or more: adults, $10; children under 18, $5.

Contact: Dignity Health Sports Park, 18400 Avalon Blvd., Carson CA 90746; (877) 604-8777.

LOS ANGELES FC / BANC OF CALIFORNIA STADIUM

Maybe you can become a part of "The 3,252" when you watch this relatively new Major League Soccer team play. There are 3,252 seats in the supporters section at the Banc of California Stadium where they play. The Los Angeles Football Club was founded only four years ago and includes such famous investors as actor Will Ferrell, basketball legend Magic Johnson, and self-help guru Tony Robbins. Unfortunately, the FC hasn't won a championship yet, but they are still young.

Website: https://www.lafc.com and https://www.bancofcaliforniastadium.com

Info: Handicapped accessible.

Contact: Los Angeles Football Club, 3939 S Figueroa St., Los Angeles CA 90037; (213) 519-9900.

SAN JOSE EARTHQUAKES / AVAYA STADIUM

Eaaaaarrrtthhhquuuaaakkkeees! The third of California's Major League Soccer teams, they have won two MLS Cup titles. They played in several stadiums, but now play in Avaya Stadium. The coolest thing about this stadium is that it has the largest sports stadium bar in America. Fit in a tour of the stadium too.

Website: https://www.sjearthquakes.com

Info: Tour hours are Monday through Friday 9 a.m. to 5 p.m. Tours are not available on Avaya Stadium Match Days. Tour cost may depend on group size: call ahead.

Contact: Avaya Stadium, 1145 Coleman Ave., San Jose CA 95110; (408) 556-7700.

PEBBLE BEACH GOLF LINKS

Fore! If you love watching Tiger Woods and Rory McIlroy, visit some of California's notable golf courses that have hosted these greats, especially Pebble Beach Golf Links. Pebble Beach has hosted many US Opens and PGA Tour events and has an incredible golf history. You can also play 18 holes just like the pros do!

Website: https://www.pebblebeach.com/golf/pebble-beach-golf-links

Contact: Pebble Beach, 1700 17-Mile Drive, Pebble Beach CA 93953; (800) 877-0597.

RACING'S DEL MAR THOROUGHBRED CLUB

Legendary singer and actor Bing Crosby was known for such hits as "White Christmas," and his roles in such movies as *Going My Way*, but you may not know that he had a love for horses. He bought his first racehorse in 1836 and was the man behind the building of Del Mar Thoroughbred Club. Spend a day at the track and place your bets or just stop by to check out some horse racing history. The Del Mar Thoroughbred Club is also going to be the location of the 2021 Breeders' Cup, so book your vacation now.

Website: https://www.dmtc.com

Contact: Del Mar Thoroughbred Club, 2260 Jimmy Durante Blvd., Del Mar CA 92014; (858) 755-1141.

SANTA ANITA PARK

Santa Anita Park opened in 1934 and such horse racing greats as Seabiscuit and Spectacular Bid have raced and won here over the years. In 1986, Santa Anita Park hosted its first Breeders' Cup and in 1990 it hosted famed jockey Bill Shoemaker's last ride. Watch the races and make sure that you take

Website: https://www.santaanita.com

Info: Free Seabiscuit tours depart at 9:45 a.m. every Saturday and Sunday during live racing seasons.

Contact: Santa Anita Park, 285 W Huntington Dr., Arcadia CA 91007; (626) 574-7223.

Did you know?: In addition to Santa Anita Park, *Seabiscuit* was filmed at Keeneland Race Course in Lexington, Kentucky, and Saratoga Race Course in Saratoga Springs, New York.

the Seabiscuit Tour. Highlights on the tour include the stable area, Seabiscuit's original barn and stall, and areas used during the filming of the 2003 movie *Seabiscuit*.

WALLY PARKS NHRA MOTORSPORTS MUSEUM

This 30,000-square-foot museum is all about hot rods, dragsters, and land speed vehicles. Located in Pomona, the museum brings visitors through the history and culture of racing with a variety of permanent and changing exhibits, and also hosts several hot rod events and reunions.

Website: https://nhramuseum.org

Info: The museum is open year-round 10 a.m. to 5 p.m. Wednesday through Sunday. Cost: adults, $12; seniors (ages 60 and older), $10; children (age 6–15), $10; active military and children 5 and under, free. Auto Club discounts and group rate available.

Contact: 101 W McKinley Ave., Pomona CA 91768; (909) 622-2133.

UNITED STATES BICYCLING HALL OF FAME

Bicycle races have drawn crowds since the late 1800s, and this hall of fame helps to honor the sport and the people who have contributed to it. In this 8,000-square-foot space, you can see a variety of historic bicycles, racing posters, awards, and clothing that the bicyclists have worn over the years.

Website: https://usbhof.org

Info: The Hall of Fame is open Wednesday 4 p.m. to 6 p.m. and Saturday 10 a.m. to 2 p.m. General admission $5; seniors (ages 55 and older) and students, $3; some bike club members free.

Contact: United States Bicycling Hall of Fame, 303 3rd St., Davis CA 95616; (530) 341-FAME (3263).

Statue Alert!

At the 1968 Summer Olympics, gold and bronze medalists Tommy Smith and John Carlos took off their sneakers and raised their fists in a black power salute to draw attention to black poverty. They were booed and received death threats for their actions, but ultimately were hailed for what they did. Their alma mater, San Jose State University, honored them with a 22-foot statue on its campus. The statue is next to Clark Hall and Tower Hall.

COLORADO

Colorado is beautiful; even if you're not a sports fan, you should visit this incredible state. Oh those Rocky Mountains! And let's not forget about Pikes Peak! But this is a sports book, so let's get talking about all the teams and museums. The list of Colorado sports teams seems to be just as long as the list of Colorado mountains.

There have been many legendary athletes who were born here, including boxing's Jack "The Manassa Mauler" Dempsey, baseball's Cy Young winner Roy Halladay, and racing's Indianapolis 500 winner Bobby Unser. Take in a Denver Broncos football game or hit the ice and see the Colorado Avalanche. If *futbol* is more your sport, the Colorado Rapids are your team to see.

Want more? Try the National Ballpark Museum and the Colorado Sports Hall of Fame and soak in some of the great sports history of the Centennial State.

COLORADO ROCKIES / COORS FIELD

The Colorado Rockies came into MLB in 1991 as an expansion franchise. They played one season at Mile High Stadium and now reside at Coors Field, the third oldest stadium in the National League. When buying your game tickets, try to snag a purple seat which is located in the 20th row, because they sit "a mile high," or 5,280 feet above sea level. The Rooftop is the hot spot at Coors Field to watch a game, where the views are incredible, but you're standing the entire time. It's open to all ticketed guests, but an additional $16 is required to enter. That price includes $6 in concession or merchandise credit.

Before the first pitch make sure you take a Coors Field tour, available Monday through Saturday. It lasts 70–80 minutes and is accessible for guests with disabilities.

> **Website:** https://www.mlb.com/rockies and https://www.mlb.com/rockies/ballpark
>
> **Info:** Coors Field tours are offered Monday through Saturday at 10 a.m., noon, and 2 p.m. When there are evening games, tours are only offered at 10 a.m. and noon. On afternoon game days there are no tours. Cost: adults, $12; seniors (ages 55 and older), $9; children (12 and under), $9.
>
> **Contact:** Coors Field, 2001 Blake St., Denver CO 80205; (303) 292-0200.

Statue Alert!

Outside of Coors Field is a statue of Branch Rickey, a former professional baseball player and executive and the man behind the signing of #42, Jackie Robinson. The Branch Rickey Award was created in his honor and is given annually to a Major League Baseball player in recognition of exceptional community service.

NATIONAL BALLPARK MUSEUM

If you're visiting Coors Field, don't miss the National Ballpark Museum, located directly across the way. Based on the personal collection of baseball fan and researcher Bruce Hellerstein, it includes bricks and seats from various stadiums as well as tickets, programs, postcards, books, and more.

Website: www.ballparkmuseum.com

Info: The museum is open Tuesday through Saturday 11 a.m. to 5 p.m.; it is closed on Sunday, Monday, and holidays. Cost: adults, $10; seniors, $5; children 16 and under and active military, free.

Contact: National Ballpark Museum, 1940 Blake St., Suite 101, Denver CO 80202; (303) 974-5835.

DENVER BRONCOS / BRONCOS STADIUM AT MILE HIGH

This NFL team is a three-time Super Bowl champion and has included such football legends as John Elway, Shannon Sharpe, Karl Mecklenburg, Floyd Little, and Terrell Davis. The Broncos play at Broncos Stadium at Mile High and fans can take tours of the stadium throughout the year. You'll see the Colorado Sports Hall of Fame (see below), the visiting team's locker room, field tunnel entrance, and the press center, among other areas.

Website: https://www.denverbroncos.com and http://broncosstadiumatmilehigh.com

Info: The tours last 75 to 90 minutes and are fully ADA accessible. For the complete tour schedule, visit their website. Cost: adults, $25; seniors, military w/ID, and children (ages 6–12), $20; children 5 and under are free with an adult (maximum 2 per paying adult).

Contact: Broncos Stadium at Mile High, 1701 Bryant St., Suite 500, Denver CO 80204; (720) 258-3888.

COLORADO SPORTS HALL OF FAME

The Colorado Sports Hall of Fame is located at Broncos Stadium at Mile High and honors many Colorado athletes who have made a mark on their respective sports. It includes exhibits on Colorado women athletes and great moments in Colorado sports, and a Kids' Zone. From here you can also take a tour of Broncos Stadium at Mile High.

Website: https://www.coloradosports.org

Info: The Hall of Fame is open to the public and is free. Its hours are Thursday through Saturday 9:30 a.m. to 3 p.m.

Contact: Colorado Sports Hall of Fame, 1701 Mile High Stadium Cir., Suite 500, Denver CO, 80204; (720) 258-3888.

COLORADO AVALANCHE / PEPSI ARENA

This NHL team has won multiple division championships and two Stanley Cups since their first year back in 1995. They play in the Pepsi Arena, so be sure to take in a game and take a behind-the-scenes tour of this incredible venue.

Website: https://www.nhl.com/avalanche and https://www.pepsicenter.com

Info: Tours are held on Monday, Wednesday, and Friday at 10 a.m., noon, and 2 p.m., and Saturday at 10 a.m. and noon. There are no tours on Sundays and holidays. Walk-in cost: adults, $10; seniors (ages 55 and older), $8; children (ages 12 and under), $8; military (w/valid ID), $5; children 2 and under, free.

Contact: Pepsi Arena, 1000 Chopper Cir., Denver CO 80204; (303) 405-1100.

DENVER NUGGETS / PEPSI ARENA

The NBA's Denver Nuggets were called the Larks when they were founded back in the 1940s, but changed their name to the Rockets before scoring their first basket. Since then, Carmelo Anthony, Dikembe Mutombo, Alex English, and Kiki Vandeweghe are just some of the legends who have played for the franchise. They currently play in the Pepsi Arena, so be sure to take in a game and buy a ticket for a behind-the-scenes tour of this incredible venue.

Website: https://www.nba.com/nuggets and https://www.pepsicenter.com

Info: Tours are held on Monday, Wednesday, and Friday at 10 a.m., noon, and 2 p.m.; Saturday at 10 a.m. and noon. There are no tours on Sundays and holidays. Walk-in cost: adults, $10; seniors (ages 55 and older) and children (ages 12 and under), $8; military (w/valid ID), $5; children 2 and under, free.

Contact: Pepsi Arena, 1000 Chopper Cir, Denver CO 80204; (303) 405-1100.

COLORADO RAPIDS / DICK'S SPORTING GOODS PARK

The Colorado Rapids were one of the first soccer clubs to form the MLS in 1996 and won the MLS Cup in 2010. They play at Dick's Sporting Goods Park in Commerce City, so enjoy the beautiful game and take a free walking tour of the park on Monday, Wednesday, and Friday (make sure you call ahead for the tour).

Website: https://www.coloradorapids.com and https://www.dickssportinggoodspark.com

Info: The free tours are offered on Monday, Wednesday, and Friday at both 10 a.m. and 2 p.m.

Contact: Dick's Sporting Goods Park, 6000 Victory Way, Commerce City CO 80022; (303) 727-3500.

> ### Good Eats
> Former Denver Broncos quarterback John Elway Jr. owns several restaurants in Vail and Denver, all under the name—what else?—Elway's. Visit https://elways.com for more information.

COLORADO SNOWSPORTS MUSEUM HALL OF FAME

You can't talk about Colorado without talking about snow and snow sports, so it's only fitting that they have a Snowsports Museum Hall of Fame. You'll see presentations and films and learn about the history of the skiing industry and the skiers and snowboarders who have made an impact on the sport.

> **Website:** https://www.snowsportsmuseum.org
>
> **Info:** The museum is open daily 10 a.m. to 6 p.m. There is no admission fee, but donations are accepted.
>
> **Contact:** Colorado Snowsports Museum, 231 S. Frontage Rd. East, Vail CO 81657; (303) 273-5810.

COLLEGE SPORTS TOUR

AIR FORCE ACADEMY / FALCON STADIUM

After every Air Force Falcon score, the cadets storm the field and do push-ups for each Air Force point on the board. It's a sight to see! Each year the Air Force Falcons—who represent the US Air Force Academy—play for the coveted Commander-in-Chief's Trophy, which is awarded to each season's winner of the American college football series among the teams of the US Military Academy (Army Black Knights), the US Naval Academy (Navy Midshipmen), and US Air Force Academy (Air Force Falcons). The Falcons currently have the most wins at 20 since its inception in 1972. They play in the Mountain West Conference of the NCAA.

> **Website:** https://goairforcefalcons.com/index.aspx?path=football
>
> **Info:** No stadium tours, but you have to see a game.
>
> **Contact:** Air Force Academy Falcon Stadium, 2169 Field House Dr., US Air Force Academy CO 80840-9500; (719) 333-4008.

UNIVERSITY OF COLORADO BUFFALOES / FOLSOM FIELD

The Colorado Buffaloes have played at Folsom Field since 1924. They have played in 28 bowl games as of 2018 and won 27 conference championships, five division championships, and a National Championship in 1990.

> **Website:** https://cubuffs.com/facilities/?id=1
>
> **Contact:** Folsom Field, 2400 Colorado Ave., Boulder CO 80302; (303) 492-9675.

COLORADO STATE UNIVERSITY RAMS / CANVAS STADIUM

Website: https://csurams.com/facilities/?id=17

Info: Canvas Stadium tours are free and scheduled through the CSU Alumni Association. You will see the Smith Alumni Center, the New Belgium Porch, the Indoor Club level, the Stadium Club level, the Markley Family Hall of Champions, and the offices for CSU Football operations. They are available Monday through Friday throughout the year. You can sign up for tours in advance by clicking the "Register" button on the website. Tour times are subject to change and tours are not available the day before or the day of a home football game.

Contact: Canvas Stadium, 751 W Pitkin St., Fort Collins CO 80521; (970) 491-5300.

CONNECTICUT

There aren't any professional sports teams in Connecticut, but that's okay because the University of Connecticut (known as UConn) has just as much excitement to keep sports fans busy. Once you're done rooting on the Huskies, then get your speed on at any one of Connecticut's racing tracks. Here you can even get behind the wheel and feel like one of the NASCAR legends!

COLLEGE SPORTS TOUR

UNIVERSITY OF CONNECTICUT / J. ROBERT DONNELLY HUSKY HERITAGE SPORTS MUSEUM

When it comes to exciting championship games and racking up NCAA titles, the Huskies are it. If you're in the area, make sure you get tickets to see either the men's or women's basketball team. The women have won an impressive 11 NCAA championships. The J. Robert Donnelly Husky Heritage Sports Museum is an entire museum dedicated to the school's sport history and is worth a visit. Tour the National Champions Gallery and see the NCAA National Championship Men's Soccer trophies; a 1931 football signed by the entire Connecticut squad; team photos of Connecticut's first men's (1901) and women's (1902) basketball squads; and the Connecticut Basketball Rotunda which has championship trophies and paintings. Watch the video wall where you can see footage of their winning moments.

> **Website:** https://uconnhuskies.com
>
> **Info:** The 2,700-square-foot museum is located in the UConn Alumni Center. It is free and open to the public Monday through Friday 8 a.m. to 5 p.m.
>
> **Contact:** University of Connecticut, Storrs CT; (860) 486-4900.

STAFFORD MOTOR SPEEDWAY

Racing fans will love Connecticut, because here you can not only watch the races, you can live out your dreams of becoming a racer. The Stafford Motor Speedway hosts NASCAR races, so plan a racing vacation while you're in the area, starting here.

> **Website:** https://www.staffordmotorspeedway.com
>
> **Info:** Race season hours from April to October are Monday through Thursday 9 a.m. to 5 p.m. and Friday 9 a.m. to the end of the race. Saturday and Sunday hours vary depending on whether there is an event. Offseason, the hours are Monday through Thursday 9 a.m. to 5 p.m. Ticket prices vary, so check the website for price information.
>
> **Contact:** Stafford Motor Speedway, 55 West St., Stafford Springs CT 06076; (860) 684-2783.

SKIP BARBER RACING SCHOOL

Do you have dreams of being the next Mario Andretti, Dale Earnhardt Jr., or Richard Petty? Maybe you just have a need for speed? The Skip Barber Racing School puts you behind the wheel and on the track with their one-, two-, or three-day racing programs. If you can't get enough of NASCAR, then this is a must do for your bucket list.

Website: https://www.skipbarber.com

Info: Prices range based on the program and the track that you choose.

Contact: Lime Rock Park, 60 White Hollow Road, Lakeville CT 06039; (866) 932-1949.

THOMPSON SPEEDWAY MOTORSPORTS PARK

And yet another motorsports park in Connecticut for racing fans to enjoy on your racing tour. Located in Thompson, Connecticut, there are annual NASCAR stock car and open wheel racing events held here, including the NASCAR Whelen Modified Tour and NASCAR Whelen All American Series.

Website: www.thompsonspeedway.com

Info: Children 12 and under free at all events in General Admission. Ticket prices vary depending on the race, so check out the website for a complete listing.

Contact: Thompson Speedway Motorsports Park, 205 E Thompson Rd., Thompson CT 06277; (860) 923-2280.

FYI: Check out the legendary Lime Rock Park in Lime Rock, Connecticut, where there are also a variety of races held throughout the year. Visit http://limerock.com for more information and a schedule of events. It's only a half-hour away from the Skip Barber Racing School, so combine your visits.

WRESTLING FYI: If you're a fan of professional wrestling like I am, you already know that Stamford, Connecticut, is home to the headquarters of World Wrestling Entertainment, otherwise known as WWE. While I want nothing more than a WWE museum, there isn't one right now and nothing really to see here. The building has tight security and even though there are a few pieces of memorabilia in the lobby, it's only enjoyed by the employees and guests. Of course, you can just take a selfie in front of the building to say you've been there, but that's about as far as you'll get. There is a National Wrestling Hall of Fame in Waterloo, Iowa (page 64), and in Stillwater, Oklahoma (page 139), and there's also the Professional Wrestling Hall of Fame in Texas (page 160). They all pay homage to professional wrestling.

Good Eats

There are many delicious places to eat in Connecticut, but you may prefer to stop by Bobby V's Restaurant and Sports Bar with locations in Stamford and Windsor Locks. They are co-owned by the former MLB player and manager Bobby Valentine. Bobby spent 10 years as a MLB player for the Dodgers, Angels, Padres, Mets, and Mariners, and also served as manager of the Rangers, Mets, and Red Sox. For more information, visit https://www.bobbyvsrestaurant.com.

DOROTHY HAMILL SKATING RINK

Dorothy Hamill was one of the first Olympic skaters America fell in love with. At the 1976 Winter Olympics in Innsbruck, Austria, Hamill came in second in the figures and then won the short and long programs, taking the gold medal. Hamill's hometown of Greenwich, Connecticut, honored her achievements with this ice rink named after her.

Website: https://www.greenwichct.gov/Facilities/Facility/Details/Dorothy-Hamill-Rink-56

Info: The rink is open from early September through mid-March.

Contact: Dorothy Hamill Rink, Sue Merz Way, Greenwich CT 06830; (203) 531-8560.

Did you know? Woodstock, Connecticut, is home to the oldest indoor bowling alley. It is located inside Roseland Cottage, the home of American businessman Henry Bowen, which is now on the National Register of Historic Places. The story goes that our 18th president, Ulysses S. Grant, bowled for the first time at this alley back in 1870. He bowled a strike and wanted to celebrate by enjoying a cigar, but Bowen made him go outside to smoke it. The cottage is open for tours Wednesday through Sunday, June 1 to October 15, from 11 a.m. to 4 p.m. Cost: adults, $10; seniors, $9; students, $5. Visit www.historicnewengland.org/property/roseland-cottage for more information.

DELAWARE

It's a small state, but you've heard that expression, "Good things come in small packages," right? Just because it's small doesn't mean you should skip it. If you did, you'd be missing the University of Delaware Blue Hens and this terrific Sports Museum and Hall of Fame.

DELAWARE SPORTS MUSEUM AND HALL OF FAME

The First State has been the native home for many professional athletes. The Delaware Sports Museum and Hall of Fame honors their contributions, so if you're in the area stop by and learn about their accomplishments. There's Dallas Green, manager of the Philadelphia Phillies squad that won the 1980 World Series, William "Judy" Johnson, who was inducted into the Baseball Hall of Fame in Cooperstown after a great career in the old Negro Leagues, and Lovett Purnell, an NFL tight end who played part of his career with the New England Patriots and went on to play in the Super Bowl.

Website: www.desports.org

Info: Open April through October. October hours are Saturday only noon to 4 p.m. Free admission.

Contact: Delaware Sports Museum and Hall of Fame, 801 Shipyard Dr., Wilmington DE 19801-5121; (302) 425-3263.

COLLEGE SPORTS TOUR

UNIVERSITY OF DELAWARE FIGHTIN' BLUE HENS / TUBBY RAYMOND FIELD AT DELAWARE STADIUM

The Delaware Fightin' Blue Hens football team has won six national titles in their 117-year history and are a must have on your college sports tour bucket list.

Website: https://bluehens.com

Contact: University of Delaware Stadium, 631 S College Ave., Newark DE 19716; (302) 831-4367.

FLORIDA

Ah, the Sunshine State is a traveler's dream. From the warm, sandy beaches to Walt Disney World, there's so much to do here. For the sports fan, the list gets even better. There's racing at the legendary Daytona International Speedway and the Homestead-Miami Speedway. Florida is also all about golf, so visit the World Golf Hall of Fame.

DAYTONA INTERNATIONAL SPEEDWAY

Call it NASCAR's Super Bowl or World Series: The Daytona International Speedway is the race of all races. Held annually in February, it's where legends such as Richard Petty, Mario Andretti, Cale Yarborough, A. J. Foyt, Michael Waltrip, Dale Earnhardt Sr., and Jeff Gordon have won. While you're here, tour the track, peek inside a Daytona 500 professional race car, or take your experience one step further with the NASCAR Racing Experience, where you can drive or be a passenger in a once-in-a-lifetime driving experience. You should also walk the Walk of Fame, where each champion's block has been imprinted with their handprint and footprint.

Website: www.daytonainternationalspeedway.com

Info: All access tours of the Speedway and museum are 90 minutes long. Cost: adults, $26; children (ages 5-12), $20; children 4 and under, free. Tours of the Speedway only are 30 minutes long. Cost: adults, $19; children (ages 5-12), $13; children 4 and under, free. There are "best value" tickets that include digital photographs that the Speedway and museum take of you while you are on the tour.

Contact: Daytona International Speedway, 1801 W International Speedway Blvd., Daytona Beach FL 32114; (800) 748-7467.

Statue Alert!

Visit the statues of NASCAR founders "Big" Bill France and Anne B. France, and racing legend Dale Earnhardt Sr., who lost his life in a crash on this track.

HOMESTEAD-MIAMI SPEEDWAY

Another NASCAR race venue where, in 2018, the Ford EcoBoost 400 saw Joey Logano win his first Monster Energy NASCAR Cup Series championship. It's where fans can see three NASCAR Championship races in one weekend. A must-see on a racing tour.

Website: www.homesteadmiamispeedway.com

Info: The Homestead-Miami Speedway offers a behind-the-scenes tour where you'll see the Champions Club, NASCAR Cup garages, Victory Lane, the spotters stand, Pit Road, and more. Tours are only available on select days, so check the calendar. Cost: $10; military and seniors, $7; children 12 and under, free.

Contact: Homestead-Miami Speedway, One Ralph Sanchez Speedway Blvd., Homestead FL 33035-1501; (305) 230-5000.

MUSEUM OF POLO AND HALL OF FAME

Marco! Oh, wait, that's not the kind of polo that is celebrated at this museum. Located in Lake Worth, the museum honors a sport which dates back to 600 BC through art, trophies, artifacts, books, periodicals, films, videos, recordings, and memorabilia.

Website: www.facebook.com/museumofpolo

Info: The Museum of Polo and Hall of Fame is open Monday through Friday 10 a.m. to 4 p.m. year-round, and during the polo season (January–April) Saturday from 10 a.m. to 2 p.m. Summer hours vary. Admission is free.

Contact: Museum of Polo and Hall of Fame, 9011 Lake Worth Road, Lake Worth FL 33467; (561) 969-3210.

WORLD GOLF HALL OF FAME

Fore! When you're at the World Golf Hall of Fame, you're honoring the greats of the game of golf, especially when you tour the 1,800-square-foot "THE PLAYERS Experience" exhibition. It's here you'll learn more about the history and champions of the game, including the legendary Arnold Palmer and the most recent champion Webb Simpson. Other exhibitions include "Major Moments: Celebrating Golf's Greatest Championships," "Honoring the Legacy: A Tribute to African-Americans in Golf," and exhibitions on the comedian and golf lover Bob Hope and the LPGA legend Nancy Lopez.

Website: www.worldgolfhalloffame.org

Info: Admission to the Hall of Fame includes entrance and one shot on the Hall of Fame Challenge Hole. The World Golf Hall of Fame and Museum is open daily and year-round except for Thanksgiving and Christmas. The Museum is open Monday through Saturday 10 a.m. to 6 p.m., Sunday noon to 6 p.m. Cost: adults, $20.95; seniors, military and Florida residents (w/valid ID), $19.95; students (ages 13 and older w/valid ID), $10; children (ages 5–12), $5; children 4 and under, free.

Contact: World Golf Hall of Fame, 1 World Golf Pl., St. Augustine FL 32092; (904) 940-4133.

HOGAN'S BEACH SHOP

Whatcha gonna do brother, when you need clothes on your trip? You're going to stop in Hogan's Beach Shop in either Orlando or Clearwater Beach and pick yourself up some souvenirs. You can also find some wrestling souvenirs too at this shop owned by the WWE's Hulk Hogan. Check out the website because sometimes Hogan schedules personal appearances.

Website: https://hogansbeachshop.com

Info: Both locations are open 10 a.m. to 9 p.m. daily.

Contact: Hogan's Beach Shop, 7679 International Dr., Orlando FL 32819; (407) 674-7457; 483 Mandalay Ave, #108, Clearwater Beach FL 33767; (727) 461-0099.

SCHRADERS LITTLE COOPERSTOWN / ST. PETERSBURG MUSEUM OF HISTORY

If you think you have a big baseball collection, you ain't seen nothin' yet. Stop by Schraders Little Cooperstown where you can see the large baseball collection certified by the *Guinness Book of World Records*. There are nearly 5,000 baseballs from baseball luminaries such as Hank Aaron, Jackie Robinson, "Shoeless" Joe Jackson, and Joe DiMaggio, and a large number of autographed team baseballs.

Website: http://spmoh.com

Info: The St. Petersburg Museum of History is open Monday through Saturday 10 a.m. to 5 p.m. and Sunday noon to 5 p.m. Cost: adults (18 and older), $15; seniors , $12; military and veterans, $9; teachers and students, $9; children (ages 7–17), $9; children 6 and under, free.

Contact: St. Petersburg Museum of History, 335 2nd Ave. NE, St. Petersburg FL 33701; (727) 894-1052.

MIAMI MARLINS / MARLINS PARK

Here's a fun fact about this MLB team—the Marlins have never won a division title, but they have won two World Series championships. In both 1997 and 2003, they did it as a wild card team.

Website: https://www.mlb.com/marlins

Info: Tours of the stadium are available, but as of this writing Marlins Park was undergoing enhancements and the new tour information was not updated.

Contact: Marlins Park, 501 Marlins Way, Miami FL 33125; (305) 480-1300.

Did you know? Babe Ruth's longest home run ever was a whopping 587 feet, hit back on April 4, 1919. There's a marker on the University of Tampa's campus that honors that momentous occasion.

TAMPA BAY RAYS / TROPICANA FIELD

The domed Tropicana Field has housed the MLB AL East team since 1998, but the Tampa Bay Rays have yet to win a World Series title. Check out a game and cheer them on! Ted Williams didn't play for the Rays—he played for the Boston Red Sox—but this is where you'll find the Ted Williams Museum and Hitters Hall of Fame (more info below).

Website: https://www.mlb.com/rays and https://www.mlb.com/rays/ballpark

Info: There are tours, but not on Rays home days, so it is not possible to combine a game with a tour. The 90-minute tours are available at 10:30 a.m. and 1:00 p.m. Tickets may be purchased online or at the Rays Republic Main Team Store. Cost: adults, $10; seniors (ages 55 and older) and military, $8; children (14 and under), $5.

Contact: Tropicana Field, 1 Tropicana Dr., St. Petersburg FL 33705; (727) 825-3137.

TED WILLIAMS MUSEUM AND HITTERS HALL OF FAME

The Museum and Hall of Fame is located at the Tampa Bay Rays' Tropicana Field, and covers the life and career of the man known as "The Kid." Ted Williams played his entire career with the Boston Red Sox, from 1939 to 1960, and retired with a whopping .344 batting average, 521 home runs, and a .482 on-base percentage, the highest of all time. Those are just a few of his baseball accomplishments.

The museum also has exhibits on the Tampa Bay Rays, the Cy Young award, the Negro Leagues, the All-American Girls Baseball League, and the Triple Crown—achieved by players such as Williams who have led the league in batting average, home runs, and runs batted in (RBI) in the same season.

Website: www.tedwilliamsmuseum.com

Info: The museum is open for two hours before all Rays home games and stays open through the sixth inning.

Contact: Ted Williams Museum and Hitters Hall of Fame, c/o Tropicana Field, 1 Tropicana Dr., St. Petersburg FL 33705; (352) 476-6042.

MIAMI HEAT / AMERICANAIRLINES ARENA

This three-time NBA championship team is fun to watch. Amazing players who have worn the Heat uniform in the past include Alonzo Mourning, Tim Hardaway, Dwyane Wade, Shaquille O'Neal, LeBron James, and Chris Bosh.

Website: https://www.nba.com/heat and https://www.aaarena.com/teams/detail/miami-heat

Contact: AmericanAirlines Arena, 601 Biscayne Blvd., Miami FL 33132; (786) 777-1000.

ORLANDO MAGIC / AMWAY CENTER

This NBA team has yet to win a championship, but at one point in its team history Shaquille O'Neal and Anfernee "Penny" Hardaway were a force to be reckoned with. Such players as Dwight Howard, Pat Garrity, and JJ Redick have also put the magic in the Magic.

Website: https://www.nba.com/magic and https://www.amwaycenter.com/events/orlando-magic

Contact: Amway Center, 400 W Church St. #200, Orlando FL 32801; (407) 440-7900.

JACKSONVILLE JAGUARS / TIAA BANK FIELD

The NFL's Jaguars were founded in 1995 and have yet to win a Super Bowl, but take in a game while you're in the area. The TIAA Bank Field does offer behind-the-scenes tours, where you can learn about their open-air amphitheater and indoor practice facility. Oh, and you'll get a close-up view of that ginormous video board—it's 60 feet high and 362 feet long!

Website: https://www.jaguars.com and https://tiaabankfield.com

Info: Behind-the-scenes stadium tours are $20 plus fees; military and first responders, $15 plus fees; seniors and children (ages 12 and under), $10 plus fees. Tours are available on Tuesday and Friday at 3 p.m. and Saturday at 10 a.m. and last approximately 60 to 90 minutes. You'll see the South End Zone, tunnel, owner's suite, press box, and other areas that typically aren't available to the general public.

Contact: TIAA Bank Field, 1 TIAA Bank Field Drive, Jacksonville FL 32202; (904) 633-6100.

MIAMI DOLPHINS / HARD ROCK STADIUM

The two-time NFL champions were founded in 1966 by attorney/politician Joe Robbie and actor and comedian Danny Thomas (Danny Thomas also founded St. Jude's Hospital—props!). Don Shula coached the Dolphins to their two Super Bowl victories, following their undefeated 1972 season and again the next year. Legendary quarterback Dan Marino spent 17 seasons with the team.

The Hard Rock Stadium is home to the Dolphins, but it's also the venue for college football's Capital One Orange Bowl, the University of Miami's Hurricanes, tennis's Miami Open, and Super Bowl LIV (2020).

Website: https://www.miamidolphins.com and https://hardrockstadium.com

Contact: Hard Rock Stadium, 347 Don Shula Dr., Miami Gardens FL 33056; (305) 943-8000.

Good Eats

Speaking of Don Shula, the former Miami Dolphins coach has a chain of steak houses that you can try on your sports travel tours. Visit www.shulas.com for a list of 25 locations across the country.

TAMPA BAY BUCCANEERS / RAYMOND JAMES STADIUM

The Buccaneers won the Super Bowl following the 2002 season and have been the team for such football greats as Jimmie Giles, John Lynch, Ronde Barber, and Warren Sapp. The Buccaneers play at Raymond James Stadium, which is also home to college football's Outback Bowl and the University of South Florida Bulls. You can take a behind-the-scenes stadium tour and get up-close to the famous Tampa Bay Buccaneers pirate ship in Buccaneers Cove. It's located behind sections 146 to 150, and the ship fires cannons after every Bucs score. They fire the cannons seven times for a touchdown, three times for a field goal, and two times for a safety. The tour also takes you to a luxury suite, the stadium clubs, the University of South Florida home team locker room, the field, and more.

Website: https://www.buccaneers.com and http://raymondjamesstadium.com

Info: Walk-up tours are offered on Monday, Tuesday, Wednesday, Thursday, and select Fridays at 2 p.m. Cost: adults, $10; seniors (ages 55 and older) and military, $8; children (ages 5-11), $7; children 4 and under, free.

Contact: Raymond James Stadium, 4201 N Dale Mabry Hwy., Tampa FL 33607; (813) .350-6500.

FLORIDA PANTHERS / BB&T CENTER

The Panthers started in the NHL in 1993 and were founded by the same guy who founded Blockbuster, Wayne Huizenga. They play at the BB&T Center, an indoor arena in Sunrise. Unfortunately the Panthers have yet to win any Stanley Cups, but you should still see a game on your NHL sports tour.

Website: https://www.nhl.com/panthers and https://www.thebbtcenter.com/arena-info

Contact: BB&T Center, 1 Panther Pkwy., Sunrise FL 33323; (954) 835-7000.

TAMPA BAY LIGHTNING / AMALIE ARENA

Tampa Bay is known as the lightning capital of North America, hence this team's name. The Lightning won one Stanley Cup back in 2004. Unfortunately lightning hasn't struck twice when it comes to winning the championship again. You should still take in a game and a tour of the arena while you're in Tampa.

Website: https://www.nhl.com/lightning and https://www.amaliearena.com

Info: On Tampa Bay Lightning game day, you can take a one-hour behind-the-scenes walking tour of the Amalie Arena—and you don't need a game ticket to take the tour. You'll see the pipe organ, press box, and Zambonis. Cost: $10, with children five and under free.

Contact: Amalie Arena, 401 Channelside Dr., Tampa FL 33602; (813) 301-2500.

MLS SOCCER

There are two MLS soccer teams in Florida—Inter Miami CF and Orlando City SC. Inter Miami CF is an expansion team that is co-owned by the legendary soccer player David Beckham. They will officially start in the MLS in 2020 and, as of this writing, no stadium location has been determined, so check for updates before your travels. If you're in the Orlando area, watch an Orlando City SC game. They play at, where else, Orlando City Stadium, which offers a 45-minute behind-the-scenes tour of the stadium where you'll see the player's locker room and walkout tunnel, the press box, owner's suite, and on-field warmup seats.

Website: https://www.orlandocitysc.com

Info: Check the website for the latest tour schedules. Cost: adults, $20; children, (ages 2–12), $12.

Contact: Orlando City Stadium, 655 W Church St., Orlando FL 32805; (407) 480-4702.

MIAMI OPEN

Martina Navratilova and Chris Evert once competed in front of a sellout crowd at the Miami Open. Andre Agassi and Monica Seles became two of the tournament's youngest champions when they played. In 2019 Roger Federer and Ashleigh Barty were the singles champions. What tennis superstar will you see at these matches which are held every March? Visit https://www.miamiopen.com for information on the next Open.

COLLEGE SPORTS TOUR

FLORIDA STATE UNIVERSITY / DOAK CAMPBELL STADIUM

Okay, full disclosure. I spent one semester as a student at Florida State University many moons ago. My favorite part of my quick time there was going to the football games. I went to two of them during that semester and, to this day, I remember them vividly and feel like I'll always be a Seminoles fan. If you want to see what all the excitement is about, you should see a football—or baseball or basketball—game too. Go 'Noles!

Website: https://seminoles.com/sports/football/#

Info: Florida State University's "The Seminole Experience" showcases FSU's athletic venues, including Doak Campbell Stadium, Dick Howser Stadium, the Seminole Softball Complex, Seminole Soccer Complex, Sod Cemetery, and the Albert J. Dunlap Athletic Training Facility. The Seminole Experience is open to the public Thursday through Sunday 11 a.m. to 6 p.m. Cost: regular admission, $20; discounted registrations are available for FSU staff/faculty, military, and first responders for $15 with a valid ID. Tickets for FSU students and Seminole Boosters are $10, and children under 2 are free.

Contact: Doak Campbell Stadium, 403 Stadium Dr., Tallahassee FL 32304; (850) 645-1318.

UNIVERSITY OF FLORIDA / BEN HILL GRIFFIN STADIUM

As a Seminoles fan I almost deleted the Gators from the book—but I'll be fair and keep them in here. If you are a member of the "Gator Nation," this is a must-stop on your college sports travel tour. You'll take in a football game at Ben Hill Griffin Stadium, which is appropriately called "The Swamp." The stadium doesn't offer any tours though.

Website: https://floridagators.com

Contact: Ben Hill Griffin Stadium, 157 Gale Lemerand Dr., Gainesville FL 32611; (352) 375-4683.

UNIVERSITY OF MIAMI HURRICANES / HARD ROCK STADIUM

It's another Seminoles rivalry team—but if you love the Hurricanes, take in a game at the Hard Rock Stadium. Like I said above, this venue is not just home to the Hurricanes, but it's also home to the NFL's Miami Dolphins, college football's Capital One Orange Bowl, tennis's Miami Open, and Super Bowl LIV (2020).

Website: https://hurricanesports.com

Contact: Hard Rock Stadium, 347 Don Shula Dr., Miami Gardens FL 33056; (305) 943-8000.

GEORGIA

This is the state where I fell in love with sweet tea, and you will too. But again, this is a sports book (just trust me on the sweet tea) and you will have plenty to do in the Peach State. There is baseball's Atlanta Braves, football's Atlanta Falcons, and basketball's Atlanta Hawks just to start. The sports history here is amazing and includes the legendary Ty Cobb. Just keep reading and Georgia will be on your mind, and you'll see even more sports history come to life.

TY COBB MUSEUM

He was known as the Georgia Peach, and this legendary baseball player was one of the best the sport has ever seen. Ty Cobb was born in Narrows, Georgia, and this museum in Royston honors his legacy, which includes being the first player elected to the National Baseball Hall of Fame and Museum in Cooperstown, New York. Check out the Ty Cobb memorial statue while you're there.

Website: https://www.tycobb.org

Info: The Museum is open Monday through Friday 9 a.m. to 4 p.m. and Saturday 10 a.m. to 4 p.m. Cost: adults, $5; seniors, $4; students and children under 5, free.

Contact: Ty Cobb Museum, 461 Cook St., Royston GA 30662; (706) 245-1825.

GEORGIA SPORTS HALL OF FAME

There are more than 400 athletes honored in the Georgia Sports Hall of Fame in Macon. The inductees in this 43,000-square-foot venue include such athletes as the New York Mets' Ray Knight, who was from Albany, and Angel Myers-Martino, an Olympian who won a multitude of medals in two Summer Olympic Games.

Website: http://georgiasportshalloffame.com/site

Info: The Hall of Fame is open Tuesday through Friday 10 am to 5 p.m., as well as 10 a.m. to 3 p.m. on Saturday, but it's closed on Sunday. Cost: adults (17 and older), $8; seniors, college students, and military (w/id), $6; children (16 and under), $3.50.

Contact: Georgia Sports Hall of Fame, 301 Cherry St., Macon GA 31201; (478) 752-1585.

GO BANANAS AT GRAYSON STADIUM

Grayson Stadium in Savannah is filled with baseball history as such legends as Babe Ruth, Lou Gehrig, Mickey Mantle, and Hank Aaron once played there. It's now home to the Savannah Bananas baseball team—what a great name!—but you can stop by and check out a game and envision the legendary greats on the field. Hey, you might also be watching a future legend there too!

Website: https://thesavannahbananas.com

Contact: Grayson Stadium, 1401 E Victory Dr., Savannah GA 31404; (912) 712-2482.

AUGUSTA NATIONAL GOLF CLUB

This beautiful course is where the best golfers in the world compete in the annual Masters Tournament, which is held every April. It's a must-see for every golf fan.

Website: /www.augusta.com

Info: You cannot play a round at Augusta National Golf Club, so try to get tickets to the tournament.

Contact: Augusta National Golf Club, 2604 Washington Rd., Augusta GA 30904; (706) 667-6000.

While the golfers are yelling "fore!" you'll be (whispering) "wow" when you see the beautiful Augusta National Golf Course. WIKIMEDIA COMMONS

ATLANTA BRAVES / SUNTRUST PARK

Talk about a storied history. The Atlanta Braves franchise started out in Boston back in 1871, moved to Milwaukee in 1953, and finally became the Atlanta Braves in 1966. The Braves have won three World Series titles since their inception, and the team has included such legendary players as Hank Aaron and pitchers Warren Spahn, Greg Maddux, and Phil Niekro.

In addition to tickets to a game, walk-up tours of SunTrust Park are offered year-round. Tickets can be purchased in advance or at the main ticket office the day of the tour. There are a limited number of tickets for each tour time, so it's best to buy in advance. You will see the Xfinity Rooftop Press Box, Hank Aaron Terrace, INFINITI Club Monument, Garden Delta SKY360° Club, and so much more.

Website: https://www.mlb.com/braves/ballpark

Info: The stadium tours are held from October to March, Monday through Saturday at 9:30 a.m., 11 a.m., 12:30 p.m., and 2 p.m., as well as April to September, Monday through Saturday at 10 a.m., 11:30 a.m., 1 p.m., and 2:30 p.m., and Sunday at 1 p.m. and 2:30 p.m. Cost: adults, $20; children (12 and under), $12; groups and military, $15.

Contact: SunTrust Park, 755 Battery Ave. SE, Atlanta GA 30339; (404) 577-9100.

ATLANTA HAWKS / STATE FARM ARENA

While the Atlanta Braves had their beginnings in Boston, the NBA's Atlanta Hawks had theirs in Buffalo, New York. They started as the Buffalo Bisons in 1946 and became the Atlanta Hawks in 1968. Unfortunately, they haven't won a championship in almost 60 years, but maybe their luck will change when you stop by and watch a game.

Website: https://www.nba.com/hawks

Contact: State Farm Arena, 1 State Farm Dr., Atlanta GA 30303; (404) 878-3000.

ATLANTA FALCONS / MERCEDES-BENZ STADIUM

The Falcons have been a team since the mid-1960s, but have not won a Super Bowl even after two appearances. At Mercedes-Benz Stadium you can enjoy a behind-the-scenes tour that includes the locker rooms and going onto the field. As of this writing, the stadium was coming up with new tour experiences, including an art tour.

Website: https://www.atlantafalcons.com and https://mercedesbenzstadium.com

Info: FYI, the Mercedes-Benz Stadium is also home to Major League Soccer's Atlanta United FC. Stadium tours are conducted daily from 11 a.m. to 4 p.m. Cost: adults, $25; children (3-12), seniors, and military, $20.

Contact: Mercedes-Benz Stadium, 1 AMB Dr. Northwest, Atlanta GA 30313; (470) 341-5000.

RACING FANS

Racing fans will love traveling to Georgia, home to approximately 22 (!) race-tracks and drag strips, including the Atlanta Motor Speedway (www.atlantamotor speedway.com), Road Atlanta (https://www.roadatlanta.com), and the Atlanta Dragway (www.atlantadragway.com). Make sure you check each website for updated racing schedules and ticket prices.

COLLEGE SPORTS TOUR

UNIVERSITY OF GEORGIA BULLDOGS

How's this for a cool stat? The Georgia Bulldogs' two Heisman winners, Frank Sinkwich and Herschel Walker, received the award 40 years apart. Both of their teams won SEC championships. So, who let the dogs out? You should be there when they play. When it comes to college football in Georgia, it's all about the rivalry between the University of Georgia Bulldogs and the Georgia Tech Yellow Jackets. It's actually dubbed "Clean, Old-Fashioned Hate." The Bulldogs play at Sanford Stadium, where the 1996 Olympic men's and women's soccer competition was also held.

Website: https://georgiadogs.com

Contact: Sanford Stadium, 100 Sanford Dr., Athens GA 30602; (706) 542-9036.

GEORGIA TECH YELLOW JACKETS / BOBBY DODD STADIUM AT HISTORIC GRANT FIELD

The Georgia Tech Yellow Jackets football team plays in Bobby Dodd Stadium at Historic Grant Field in Atlanta and have won four national championships (1917, 1928, 1952, 1990) and 16 conference titles.

Website: https://ramblinwreck.com/sports/m-footbl/ and https://ramblinwreck.com/bobby-dodd-stadium

Contact: Bobby Dodd Stadium, 177 N Ave. NW, Atlanta GA 30313; (404) 894-9645.

HAWAII

There aren't any professional sports teams in Hawaii, but college sports fans and surfing fans will still want to visit the islands (okay, honestly, I don't need an excuse to visit Hawaii, but if you need one I have a few for you). Here you can catch a game with the University of Hawaii's Rainbow Warriors at the Aloha Stadium, which was home to the NFL's Pro Bowl for many years as well as the NCAA's Hula Bowl. If you didn't already know, Hawaii is also the birthplace of surfing, and you might just catch a professional surfing competition.

COLLEGE SPORTS TOUR

UNIVERSITY OF HAWAII'S RAINBOW WARRIORS / ALOHA STADIUM

Aloha Stadium is home to the University of Hawaii's Rainbow Warriors. The stadium offers a 60- to 90-minute behind-the-scenes tour that includes the South Corridor Museum, Skybox, upper-level seating, press box, locker rooms, and the field.

Website: http://alohastadium.hawaii.gov

Info: At the time of this writing, the stadium offered free field photo ops on certain days/times, so check the website to see if this perk is still available. Cost: adults, $7; seniors, military (w/ID), and children (ages 4–12), $5; ; children 3 and under, free (must be accompanied by a paying adult).

Contact: Aloha Stadium, 99-500 Salt Lake Blvd., Honolulu HI 96818; (808) 483-2500.

IDAHO

Idaho is a "gem" of a state for the sports fan to visit (more than 70 different precious and semi-precious gemstones have been found there). You probably know it as the Potato State, but what's most important is that it's home to the Boise State Broncos, a team which should get your support while you're here.

COLLEGE SPORTS TOUR

BOISE STATE BRONCOS / ALBERTSONS STADIUM

When Boise State's stadium was due for a makeover, athletic director Gene Bley-maier realized that the school was spending $750,000 to pull up an old green carpet and put down a new green carpet, and nobody was going to notice or care. Knowing that everyone knew it was artificial turf, he decided to put down the school color—blue—instead of the traditional green. Now, it's a popular tourist attraction and visitors come from all around the world to snap a selfie with the blue field. Albertsons Stadium is also home to the Famous Idaho Potato Bowl.

> **Website:** https://broncosports.com/facilities and famousidahopotatobowl.com
>
> **Contact:** 1910 University Dr., Boise ID 83725-0001; 208-426-4737.

There are two additional NCAA colleges that you can visit on your tour of the state. The University of Idaho Vandals play at the Kibbie Dome in Moscow (yes, in Idaho) and the Idaho State Bengals play at Holt Arena, an indoor facility on campus in Pocatello. Visit www.uidaho.edu and https://isubengals.com for more information.

ILLINOIS

When I spent a week in Chicago for the very first time, it was cold! But I loved every second of it: the arts, the pizza, and of course the sports. Illinois is home to the Chicago Bears football team, Chicago Blackhawks hockey team, Chicago Bulls basketball team, Chicago Cubs and Chicago White Sox baseball teams, and the Chicago Fire soccer team.

CHICAGO SPORTS MUSEUM

This huge 23,000-square-foot museum on Chicago's Magnificent Mile honors the Chicago teams and the legends who have paved the way. But it's not just about looking at memorabilia. Here you experience interactive exhibits that let you score goals like a Chicago Blackhawks player, shoot free throws like a member of the Bulls, and compare the size of William "Refrigerator" Perry's Super Bowl ring to yours (his is the largest ever made so don't expect to come too close). And "Curses!", there is an entire section devoted to Chicago's superstitions, especially the Cubs' famous 108-year drought.

> **MONEY-SAVING TIP:** If you have a meal at the nearby Harry Caray's 7th Inning Stretch (www.harrycarays .com/harry-carays-7th-inning-stretch-mag-mile.html), you will receive a complimentary admission to the museum with minimum purchase ($10 adults, $6 children and seniors).

Website: https://www.chicagosportsmuseum.com

Info: The museum is open Monday through Thursday 11:30 a.m. to 8:30 p.m., Friday 11:30 a.m. to 9:00 p.m., Saturday 11 a.m. to 9 p.m., and Sunday 11 a.m. to 6 p.m. Cost: general admission (ages 12–64), $10; seniors and children (ages 4–11), $6; children 3 and under, free.

Contact: Chicago Sports Museum, Water Tower Place, Level 7, 835 N Michigan Ave., Chicago IL 60611; (312) 202-0500.

COLLEGE SPORTS TOUR

There are several Illinois colleges that are must-sees on your college sports tours. Here are the websites for each of them:

University of Illinois Fighting Illini: https://fightingillini.com
Loyola University Ramblers: https://loyolaramblers.com
Illinois State Redbirds: https://goredbirds.com
Northern Illinois Huskies: https://niuhuskies.com

CHICAGO BEARS / SOLDIER FIELD

"Da Bears" have been in existence for 100 years. They were established on September 17, 1920, and since then there have been some amazing players who have worn a Bears uniform, including Walter Payton, Dick Butkus, Brian Piccolo, Gale Sayers, and Mike Ditka. They won their only championship by defeating the New England Patriots in Super Bowl XX following the 1985 season. They currently play at Soldier Field, which has an incredible history that goes beyond the Bears. Such great athletes as Jesse Owens, Jack Dempsey, and David Beckham have also played there. Your 60- to 75-minute behind-the-scenes tour includes going on the field just like they have, the visitors' locker room, interview room, and the VIP suites.

Website: https://soldierfield.net

Info: Cost: Classic Tour pricing: adults (ages 19–59), $15; students (ages 6–18), seniors (ages 60 and older) and military (w/id), $10; children 5 and under, $5. Visit the website for Classic Tour dates.

Contact: Soldier Field, 1410 Museum Campus Dr., Chicago IL 60605; (312) 235-7000.

CHICAGO BLACKHAWKS / UNITED CENTER

So let's talk about "6" when it comes to the NHL's Blackhawks. They were founded in 1926 as part of the "Original Six"—along with the Detroit Red Wings, Montreal Canadiens, Toronto Maple Leafs, Boston Bruins, and New York Rangers. They have won six Stanley Cup championships too. You can watch them play at the United Center.

Website: https://www.nhl.com/blackhawks

Contact: United Center, 901 W Madison St., Chicago IL 60612; (312) 455-4500.

Statues Alert!
Get your cameras out for a selfie with the statues of the NHL greats Bobby Hull and Stan Mikita outside of the United Center, home of the Chicago Blackhawks.

CHICAGO BULLS / UNITED CENTER

Founded in 1966, the Chicago Bulls have won six championships. One of the greatest NBA playersof all time, Michael Jordan, played for the Bulls for most of his 15-season career.

You can watch them play at the United Center.

Website: https://www.nba.com/bulls

Contact: United Center, 901 W Madison St., Chicago IL 60612; (312) 455-4500.

CHICAGO FIRE / SEAT GEEK STADIUM

MLS's Chicago Fire won their first MLS Cup the first season they started—in 1997. They were named after the Great Chicago Fire of 1871. After playing in Soldier Field for three years, they now play at Seat Geek Stadium.

Website: https://www.chicago-fire.com

Contact: Seat Geek Stadium, 7000 S Harlem Ave., Bridgeview IL 60455; (708) 594-7200.

CHICAGO CUBS / WRIGLEY FIELD

You can't talk about baseball's Chicago Cubs without talking about the curse that followed them for 108 years. It was broken in 2016 when the Cubs won the World Series. They play out of Wrigley Field, which is named after chewing gum magnate William Wrigley Jr. You can take a 75- to 90-minute tour of the stadium both on game days and non–game days; you can see the seating bowl, press box (not on game day), visitors' locker room (not on game day), the Cubs' dugout (not on game day), the famous ivy-covered wall, and the field.

Website: https://www.mlb.com/cubs

Info: Cost of standard non–game day and game day tours, $25; children 2 and under, free. Non–game day Ivy Tours, $35; children 2 and under, free. Ivy Tours include the opportunity to take a photo in front of the legendary ivy-covered outfield wall.

Contact: Wrigley Field. 1060 W Addison, Chicago IL 60613; (800) THE-CUBS.

Good Eats

There's so much to see and do in Illinois, especially Chicago, that you'll need some good meals to keep you going. Luckily for the sports fan, there are restaurants owned by legendary Chicago sports figures for you to try:

HARRY CARAY: The legendary sportscaster had a very lengthy career calling games for the St. Louis Cardinals, St. Louis Browns, and Oakland Athletics. He spent his last 26 years in Chicago, calling games for the White Sox and the Cubs. Visit https://www.harrycarays.com for all the restaurant locations and menus.

MICHAEL JORDAN: He flew through the air with the greatest of ease and now owns multiple Illinois restaurants, including Michael Jordan's Steak House Chicago and Michael Jordan's Restaurant. Visit http://mjshchicago.com and https://michaeljordansrestaurant.com for more information.

MIKE DITKA: As the former coach of the Chicago Bears, "Iron" Mike Ditka led Da Bears to a victory in Super Bowl XX and was named NFL Coach of the Year twice (1985, 1988). His culinary venture is Ditka's Restaurants, with locations in Chicago, Oakbrook Terrace, Westmont, and Ditka's hometown of Pittsburgh, Pennsylvania. Visit www.ditkasrestaurants.com for locations, hours, and menus.

CHICAGO WHITE SOX / GUARANTEED RATE FIELD

While the Chicago Cubs play in the MLB's National League, the Chicago White Sox play in the American League. They have won three World Series in their franchise history. They play at Guaranteed Rate Field, which was once called Comiskey Park.

Website: https://www.mlb.com/whitesox

Info: Tours of Guaranteed Rate Field are available on weekdays only with advance reservations. Tours begin at 10:30 a.m. on game days and 10:30 a.m. and 1:30 p.m. on non-game days. They include the home dugout, the press box, the field, the suites, and the Stadium Club.

Contact: Guaranteed Rate Field, 333 W 35th St., Chicago IL 60616; (312) 674-1000.

INDIANA

Did you know that Indiana is known for its Pierogi Fest? What does that have to do with sports? Nothing really. But if you're looking for sports, then let's talk about NASCAR's Indianapolis 500, the race of all races. Oh, and then there is a little thing called Hoosiers basketball, which is the spirit and the heart of Indiana college sports.

MASCOT HALL OF FAME

The Mascot Hall of Fame in Whiting honors those costumed cheerleaders who make games so much fun. Some of the mascots already inducted include Mr. Met of the New York Mets, the Phillie Phanatic of the Philadelphia Phillies, and Bucky the Badger from the University of Wisconsin.

Website: https://mascothalloffame.com

Info: The museum shares space with a children's museum. It is open on Monday, Tuesday, Wednesday, Friday, and Saturday 10 a.m. to 6 p.m., Thursday 10 a.m. to 8 p.m., and Sunday 10 a.m. to 5 p.m. Cost: $12; teachers and seniors, $10; active military and children 2 and under, free.

Contact: Mascot Hall of Fame, 1851 Front St., Whiting IN 46394; (219) 354-8814.

INDIANA BASKETBALL HALL OF FAME

From the 6,000 engraved bricks with the names of the Indiana teams, coaches, and players, to the special sections dedicated to John Wooden, Oscar Robertson, Larry Bird, and the 1954 Milan Indians, there is so much to see at this 14,000-square-foot sports museum and hall of fame in New Castle. Check out the jerseys, trophies, and photos; test your knowledge of Indiana trivia; or become a sportscaster on "You Make the Call."

Website: https://www.hoopshall.com

Info: The Indiana Basketball Hall of Fame museum is open Monday through Saturday 10 a.m. to 5 p.m. year-round and Sunday 1 p.m. to 5 p.m. March through November. Closed on Sunday in December, January, and February. Handicapped accessible. Cost: adults and teens, $5; children (ages 5–12), $3; children 4 and under, free.

Contact: Indiana Basketball Hall of Fame, One Hall of Fame Ct., New Castle IN 47362; (765) 529-1891.

NATIONAL ART MUSEUM OF SPORT

Now this is a cool museum. The National Art Museum of Sport combines sport with art, and here you'll see some awesome artwork portraying legendary athletes like Arthur Ashe, Muhammad Ali, and Jackie Robinson—as well as some artwork created by the athletes themselves.

Website: https://www.childrensmuseum.org/exhibits/namos

Info: Visit the website for each season's hours of operation. Cost: adults (ages 18–59), $25.75; youth (ages 2–17), $20.75; seniors (ages 60 and older), $24.50. You can enjoy the museum at a discount from 4 to 8 p.m. on the first Thursday of every month, when tickets are $5 for all.

Contact: National Art Museum of Sport, 3000 N Meridian St., Indianapolis IN 46208; (317) 334-4000.

LEAGUE STADIUM (*A LEAGUE OF THEIR OWN*)

So if you haven't heard of the movie *A League of Their Own* and you call yourself a sports fan, then you have a job to do and that's to go watch it *right now.* And remember, "there's no crying in baseball." But go ahead and laugh. The film starred the legendary Tom Hanks, Geena Davis, and Madonna. Hanks plays Jimmy Dugan, a washed-up ballplayer whose big-league days have ended. After the men go to war, Dugan decides to coach in the All-American Girls Baseball League of 1943. It's a fantastic movie and one that you can watch as a family.

League Stadium opened in 1894 and was renovated in 1991 just for the filming of the movie. Take a walk around and you will feel transported back to the film.

The stadium is also home to the DC Bombers, a summer collegiate baseball team.

Website: http://dcbombers.com

Info: Free admission, unless you're seeing a DC Bombers game too, which you really should.

Contact: League Stadium, 203 S Cherry St., Huntingburg IN 47542; (812) 683-2211.

INDIANAPOLIS 500 / INDIANAPOLIS MOTOR SPEEDWAY

Get your race on with 200 laps and 500 miles at the Indianapolis Motor Speedway. The annual Indianapolis 500 is held over Memorial Day weekend and is nicknamed the "Greatest Spectacle in Racing." Here you can see some of the best racers in the sport compete to become number one. You can also take a one-hour guided tour of the speedway and purchase an on-track experience. The Speedway also has its own

Indianapolis 500 Museum, which is right on the grounds. You can see where drivers are honored, look at artifacts and, of course, check out automobiles from NASCAR, Formula One, American short-track racing, and drag racing, as well as motorcycles.

Website: https://www.indianapolismotorspeedway.com and https://indyracingmuseum.org

Info: There are many different ticket pricing options for the Indianapolis 500, so visit the website for more information. Tours are offered from March through October 9 a.m. to 5 p.m., November to February, 10 a.m. to 4 p.m. The Indianapolis Motor Speedway Museum is open every day of the year except for Thanksgiving and Christmas. Members are free. Cost: adults, $10; youth (ages 6–15), $8; children 5 and under, free.

Contact: Indianapolis 500 / Indianapolis Motor Speedway, 4750 W 16th St., Speedway IN 46224; (317) 492-6784.

COLLEGE SPORTS TOUR

UNIVERSITY OF NOTRE DAME FIGHTING IRISH / NOTRE DAME STADIUM

Many books have been written about the University of Notre Dame Fighting Irish, starting back with its legendary football coaches Knute Rockne and Lou Holtz and continuing to today. Whether you are a fan of the Fighting Irish or not, you should take in a game and tour the stadium if you're in the area. By the way, did you know about Marshmallow Mayhem? It's when students take bags of marshmallows and throw them at each other before the game. It's tradition!

Website: https://und.com

Info: Want to walk on Notre Dame's field? Take a behind-the-scenes stadium tour, but check the website first for the updated schedule. Cost: adults, $20; youth (18 and under), seniors (ages 55 and older), military and emergency service personnel (police, fire, EMT), Notre Dame faculty/staff, and Notre Dame, St. Mary's, and Holy Cross students, $15.

Contact: Notre Dame Stadium, Moose Krause Circle, Notre Dame IN 46556; (574) 631-5000.

Did you know? The 1993 film *Rudy* is an iconic sports movie about Daniel "Rudy" Ruettiger, who overcame many obstacles to play for Notre Dame.

Statue Alert!

Indiana native and legendary coach John Wooden is immortalized in a bronze sculpture at the corner of Georgia and Meridian Streets.

INDIANA UNIVERSITY HOOSIERS

Whether you see hoops or football, take the time to enjoy being a Hoosiers fan. See a basketball game at Simon Skjodt Assembly Hall or a football game at Memorial Stadium—the choice is yours.

Website: https://iuhoosiers.com

Info: The school offers free guided tours of Cook Hall, Memorial Stadium, and Simon Skjodt Assembly Hall. You can see five national championship trophies, pieces of Indiana basketball history, ten interactive touch screens, the Indiana basketball memories collection, and the Mark Cuban Center.

Contact: Simon Skjodt Assembly Hall, 1001 E 17th St., Bloomington IN 47408; (812) 855-4848. Memorial Stadium, 1001 E 17th St., Bloomington IN 47408; (812) 855-1966.

Sports Film Facts: *Hoosiers*

The 1986 sports fim *Hoosiers* has been called one of the most inspirational films ever made and was ranked #13 on the list of best inspirational films by the American Film Institute. The film is loosely based on the story of the Milan High School basketball team that won a state championship. Gene Hackman stars as Milan's coach Norman Dale and the film costars Barbara Hershey (as Myra Fleener) and Dennis Hopper (who earned an Oscar nod for his performance as Shooter Flatch).

There are a few things that *Hoosiers* fans can do in Indiana. First, head on over to the Milan 54 Museum, which opened in 2013 and honors the boys behind the story and is home to *Hoosiers* memorabilia. Their collection includes uniforms of the team and the opposing team, as well as Myra Fleener's "Betty Rose" vintage coat, shorts, Chuck Taylor shoes, warmups, pullovers, cheerleader outfits, and much more.

Once you're done with the museum, take a one-hour drive over to Knightstown, where you can walk on the floor of the historic Hoosier Gym and buy memorabilia and feel the connection to the historic movie.

WEBSITE: http://milan54.org and http://thehoosiergym.com

INFO: The Milan 54 Museum is open Wednesday through Saturday 10 a.m. to 4 p.m. and Sunday noon to 4 p.m. The Hoosier Gym hours are 9 a.m. to 5 p.m.

CONTACT: Milan 54 Hoosiers Museum, 201 W Carr St., Milan IN 47031; Hoosier Gym, 355 N Washington St., Knightstown IN 46148; (800) 668-1895.

INDIANAPOLIS COLTS / LUCAS OIL STADIUM

This NFL team was once called the Baltimore Colts, but moved to Indianapolis in 1984. They have won one Super Bowl in Baltimore and one in Indianapolis. The legendary quarterback Johnny Unitas played for Baltimore and for 52 years he held the record for most consecutive games with a touchdown pass. It was broken in 2012 by Drew Brees. Take the 90-minute stadium tour and see the playing field, locker room, press box, and more.

Website: https://www.colts.com

Info: Tours are typically conducted at 11 a.m., 1 p.m., and 3 p.m. Monday through Friday (excluding event days and holidays). Cost: adults, $15; seniors, children (ages 4–12), and military (retired or active w/ID), $12.

Contact: Indianapolis Colts, 500 S Capitol Ave., Indianapolis IN 46225; (317) 262-8600.

INDIANA PACERS / BANKERS LIFE FIELDHOUSE

The Pacers haven't won an NBA championship, but they have had legendary ballers Paul George, Rik Smits, and Reggie Miller on their team. They play in Bankers Life Fieldhouse where fans can take a behind-the-scenes tour.

Website: https://www.nba.com/pacers

Info: The average tour will range from 30 to 45 minutes, though the length will vary based on the group. Tours are on Monday, Wednesday, and Friday at 10 a.m. and 1 p.m. Cost: adults, $4.50; teachers, $4; seniors and children (ages 5–18), $3.50; students, $2.50.

Contact: Bankers Life Fieldhouse, 125 S Pennsylvania St., Indianapolis IN 46204; (317) 917-2727.

IOWA

It's all about the farmland for the residents of the great state of Iowa, but of course it's about rooting on the Hawkeyes too! Traveling to this great state is a must for sports fans, especially those who have seen the *Field of Dreams* movie, which was shot here. And wait till you read about a wonderful Iowa Hawkeyes tradition.

FIELD OF DREAMS FARM

The Lansing Family Farm in Dyersville, Iowa, was the site of the famous 1989 baseball movie that starred Kevin Costner, Ray Liotta, and James Earl Jones, and is responsible for the famous movie line, "If you build it, they will come."

Field of Dreams is an adaptation of W. P. Kinsella's novel *Shoeless Joe*. Ray Kinsella (played by Costner) is an Iowa farmer who, while walking through his cornfields, hears a voice whispering to him, "If you build it, they will come." He continued hearing this before finally seeing a vision of a baseball diamond in his field.

It was a cold day in late December 1987 when a volunteer with the Dubuque Chamber of Commerce (working in conjunction with the Iowa Film Board), Sue Reidel, knocked on the door of the Lansing Family Farm bringing Don Lansing to his feet. Reidel would explain that they were looking for a location for their movie and asked if they could have permission. And the rest is cinematic history.

Website: www.fodmoviesite.com

Info: The farm is open daily January through October. In November, the site is open on weekends only. Several events are held each year. For example, the Ghost Sunday Comedy Show lets visitors watch the Ghost Players emerge from the magical corn to entertain the crowd with comedy.

Contact: Field of Dreams Farm, 28995 Lansing Rd., Dyersville IA 52040; (888) 875-8404.

COLLEGE SPORTS TOUR

IOWA HAWKEYES

You can't help but be a fan, if only a temporary one, of the Iowa Hawkeyes, especially when you find out about one of their school traditions. The University of Iowa's Stead Family Children's Hospital overlooks Kinnick Stadium, where the Hawkeyes play their football games. Stay in your seat at the end of the first quarter, because that's when everybody in the stadium turns and waves up to the young patients of the hospital and their families, who are sitting in their own "press box" on the top

Website: https://hawkeyesports.com/facilities

Contact: Kinnick Stadium, 825 Stadium Dr., Iowa City IA 52240; (319) 335-9327.

floor of the hospital. A simple gesture means so much and makes a simple college football game so much more special. It is incredible to be a part of that tradition.

NATIONAL WRESTLING HALL OF FAME DAN GABLE MUSEUM

There are two National Wrestling Hall of Fame locations—the other is in Stillwater, Oklahoma. The Iowa location is named after Danny Mack "Dan" Gable, an Olympic gold medalist wrestler. There is information on wrestling throughout the ages as well as exhibits on amateur and Olympic wrestling.

Website: https://nwhof.org

Contact: National Wrestling Hall of Fame Dan Gable Museum, 303 Jefferson St., Waterloo IA 50701; (319) 233-0745.

KANSAS

We're not in Kansas anymore—wait, we are! And that's a good thing because Kansas is chock-filled with awesome college sports teams, like the Kansas Jayhawks and the Kansas State Wildcats. Racing fans will love the Kansas Speedway and *futbol* fans will want to see Sporting KC take the pitch. If you're looking for the Kansas City Royals or Chiefs, remember to look in Missouri's listings.

KANSAS SPORTS HALL OF FAME

Located at the Wichita Boathouse, the Kansas Sports Hall of Fame covers Kansas sports history, including various high school and college sports records.

Website: https://www.kshof.org

Info: Hours are Monday through Friday 10 a.m. to 4 p.m. Closed Saturday and Sunday. Cost: free.

Contact: Kansas Sports Hall of Fame, Wichita Boathouse, 515 S Wichita, Wichita KS 67202; (316) 262-2038.

COLLEGE SPORTS TOUR

KANSAS JAYHAWKS

Here's an interesting sports factoid—the first coach of the Kansas Jayhawks actually invented the game of basketball. His name was James Naismith (check out the Naismith Basketball Hall of Fame in Massachusetts on page 82) and his legacy continues on as the Jayhawks men's basketball program is one of the most successful programs in the NCAA. They play at Allen Fieldhouse.

Website: https://kuathletics.com

Contact: Allen Fieldhouse, 1651 Naismith Dr., Lawrence KS 66044; (785) 864-8200.

KANSAS STATE WILDCATS / BRAMLAGE COLISEUM

Archrivals of the Kansas Jayhawks, the Kansas State Wildcats played their first season in 1902 and have since appeared in 31 NCAA basketball tournaments. They play at Bramlage Coliseum, otherwise known as "The Octagon of Doom," since K-State has won nearly 73 percent of its home games in its history, including 76 percent since moving to their current venue. Behind-the-scenes tours of select K-State Athletics facilities are conducted by Ahearn Fund Athletic Hospitality staff.

Website: www.ahearnfund.com/events/tours and https://www.kstatesports.com

Info: All tours are $50 per group of 25 people or less and $100 per group for more than 25 people. There is some limited availability on tour times so be sure to visit the website before traveling to Kansas State.

Contact: Bramlage Stadium, 1800 College Ave., Manhattan KS 66502; (785) 532-2876.

KANSAS SPEEDWAY

This racetrack was opened in 1999 and hosts many NASCAR races. You can enjoy a race by just sitting in the stands or you can take your experience up to the VIP level and purchase a fan pass that lets you walk through the garage before the race and have access to areas where other fans can't walk.

Website: www.kansasspeedway.com

Info: Single-race tickets start at $64. Ticket packages are available including four-race season packages, which start at $159 and include all four races and a Pre-Race Pass. Children 12 and under are free with an accompanying adult to all NASCAR Camping World Truck Series and NASCAR XFINITY Series races.

Contact: Kansas Speedway, 400 Speedway Blvd., Kansas City KS 66111; (866) 460-7223.

SPORTING KC

Sporting KC is one of the most popular MLS teams in the United States, selling out almost all of its games each year. They have won two MLS championships, in 2000 and 2013. There is a waitlist for season tickets, but you might be able to snag some individual tickets to a game when you're in the area. Their pitch is Children's Mercy Park, which offers behind-the-scenes tours where you can see the player locker rooms, press areas, team benches, and, of course, the pitch.

Website: https://www.sportingkc.com and https://www.sportingkc.com/childrens-mercy-park

Info: Tours are $10 per person and are offered year-round. Tours last 1–2 hours.

Contact: One Sporting Way, Kansas City KS 66111; (913) 387-3400.

KENTUCKY

And they're off! It's Kentucky and it's all about horse racing. No it's not. How can I forget that it's also about March Madness. It's about baseball, and it's about the greatest, Muhammad Ali! But the Kentucky Derby in Louisville at Churchill Downs is held the first Saturday of May and really draws a crowd. Plan early if you hope to get to the Derby because with any major event like this, hotels are booked up way in advance. And although many sports fans love beer and hot dogs at sporting events, 95 percent of the world's best bourbon is made here. While you're visiting, don't forget to taste some.

COLLEGE SPORTS TOUR

LOUISVILLE CARDINALS / KFC YUM! CENTER

College basketball fun isn't just limited to March Madness—although what a month! Check out the University of Louisville Cardinals, a team with an extensive NCAA tournament appearance history. And speaking of basketball history, visit The Yum Cardinal Basketball Hall of Champions, located on the campus in Freedom Hall. You will see memorabilia, exhibits, and an interactive trivia game.

Website: https://www.kfcyumcenter.com

Info: The Yum Cardinal Basketball Hall of Champions is free admission for all. It's open during Cardinals basketball games.

Contact: KFC Yum! Center, 1 Arena Plaza, Louisville KY 40202; (502) 690-9000.

UNIVERSITY OF KENTUCKY WILDCATS / RUPP ARENA

When you think of great college basketball teams, the University of Kentucky Wildcats immediately come to mind. They've won so much over the years and are such a great team that even if you're not a UK fan, you should try to snag some tickets to a game. While you're there, take a look around because some very notable people might be in the stands, including Drake, Jay Z, Ashley Judd, and President Obama, who have clearly vocalized their love of the team.

Website: https://www.rupparena.com and https://ukathletics.com

Info: There are no public tours of Rupp Arena, but there's a window that overlooks the lower bowl and you can take a peek inside of it when you're there. To do this, Rupp Arena's instructions are: "come to the Lexington Center Corporate Offices on the second level of the Shops at Lexington Center. Say a quick hello to our receptionist and sign in at the desk, walk through our hall of fame, and you'll find a viewing window where you can get a sneak peak inside of the arena." The window access is available Monday through Friday 9 a.m. to 5 p.m. Call ahead to make sure the window isn't blocked.

Contact: Rupp Arena, 430 West Vine St., Lexington KY 40507; (859) 233-4567.

KENTUCKY DERBY / CHURCHILL DOWNS

The Kentucky Derby is held each May in Louisville, where you get to see the best of the best in horse racing square off to see who is named, well, the best of the best. Whether you call it "The Run for the Roses" or "The Most Exciting Two Minutes in Sports," it's a horse racing fan's dream to go to the Derby (don't forget your fanciest hat!) and watch the horses race around the historic Churchill Downs track.

You can also take walking tours of the racetrack, and there is a Kentucky Derby Museum where you can check out exhibits about the race's history and learn more about the jockeys and horses. There's so much to do when it's Kentucky Derby season including the Kentucky Derby Festival, but there are also races at other times of the year, so check out the website for the complete schedule. Make sure you have a traditional mint julep while you are there.

Website: https://www.kentuckyderby.com and https://www.derbymuseum.org

Info: Kentucky Derby Museum's summer hours are from March 15 to November 30, Monday through Saturday 8 a.m. to 5 p.m and Sunday 11 a.m. to 5 p.m. In the winter (December 1–March 14), hours are Monday through Saturday 9 a.m. to 5 p.m. and Sunday 11 a.m. to 5 p.m. Cost: adults (ages 15–64), $15; seniors, $14; children (ages 5–14), $8; children 5 and under, free. Visit the Derby's website for more information on race ticket prices.

Contact: Kentucky Derby Museum, 704 Central Ave., Louisville KY 40208; (502) 637-1111. Churchill Downs, 700 Central Ave., Louisville KY 40208; (502) 636-4400.

Did you know? Famous colt Barbaro tragically shattered his leg in the 2006 Preakness and that ended his chances of winning the Triple Crown of thoroughbred racing. He is buried under the statue of him at the Kentucky Derby Museum.

KENTUCKY HORSE PARK

You can't have the races without the horses and Kentucky Horse Park celebrates these magnificent creatures. It's here where you can see the International Museum of the Horse, the Saddlebred Museum, and the Al-Marah Arabian Horse Galleries and learn about their history around the globe. You can also check out their horse shows and other equestrian events.

Website: https://kyhorsepark.com

Contact: Kentucky Horse Park, 4089 Iron Works Pkwy., Lexington KY 40511; (859) 233-4303.

LOUISVILLE SLUGGER MUSEUM AND FACTORY

The Louisville Slugger company has been making baseball bats since 1884. Now you can see exactly how it's done, and you'll get a free miniature Louisville Slugger souvenir bat to take home. Plus, you can check out the company's history at the Louisville Slugger Museum. See the vault with 3,000 bats that date back almost 100 years and the ones used by baseball legends Ted Williams and Babe Ruth. Greeting you when you come to the museum is the world's largest baseball bat, which weighs a whopping 68,000 pounds and towers 120 feet into the sky!

Website: https://www.sluggermuseum.com

Info: The museum is open Monday through Saturday 9 a.m. to 5 p.m., Sunday 11 a.m. to 5 p.m. Cost: adults, $15; seniors (ages 60 and older), $14; children (ages 6–12) $8; children 5 and under, free.

Contact: Louisville Slugger Museum and Factory, 800 W Main St., Louisville KY 40202; (877) 775-8443.

Batter up! It's the Louisville Slugger Museum in Louisville, Kentucky.
WIKIMEDIA COMMONS

The Muhammad Ali Center in Louisville, Kentucky WIKIMEDIA COMMONS

MUHAMMAD ALI CENTER

Muhammad Ali, born in Louisville, was one of the greatest boxers of all time, but there was so much more to this legend than what you saw in the ring. Ali's philanthropy took him across the globe delivering food and medical supplies, visiting soup kitchens and hospitals, and helping many charitable organizations. The Muhammad Ali Center is worth a visit to see the exhibits on social change, youth rights, and more.

Website: https://alicenter.org

Info: The Center is open on Sunday noon to 5 p.m. and Tuesday through Saturday 9:30 a.m. to 5 p.m. Closed on Monday. Cost: adults, $14; seniors, $13; military and students w/ID, $10.

Contact: Muhammad Ali Center, 144 N Sixth St., Louisville KY 40202; (502) 584-9254.

Statue Alert!

Stop by at the corner of Hancock and Lampton Streets in Louisville and see the 12-foot stainless steel sculpture of two boxing gloves overlapping to form a heart that honors Muhammad Ali's career. For a list of other Ali landmarks in Louisville, visit https://louisvilleky.gov/government/alis-louisville/ali-art-and-landmarks.

KENTUCKY SPEEDWAY

Horses aren't the only thing that they race in Kentucky! The Kentucky Speedway was founded in 1998 and has since hosted many NASCAR events. For a list of races and ticket packages, visit the Speedway's website.

Website: https://www.kentuckyspeedway.com

Contact: Kentucky Speedway, 1 Speedway Dr., Sparta KY 41086; (859) 578-2300.

LOUISIANA

This state is a melting pot of both culture and sports. That makes it one of our favorite places to visit. From the jazz of New Orleans and especially Bourbon Street and the French Quarter to the Louisiana Bulldogs and the New Orleans Saints, there's so much to do. Let's not forget all of the horse races too.

Louisiana is home to many famous athletes—including wide receiver Odell Beckham Jr., who left the New York Giants and now plays with the Cleveland Browns. He was born in Baton Rouge and played for Louisiana State University (LSU). The now-retired Peyton Manning was born in New Orleans and played quarterback for the Indianapolis Colts.

Bottom line—this southeastern state is a *must* visit for any sports fan—and any traveler actually.

COLLEGE SPORTS TOUR

Louisiana has quite a few colleges that deserve some time and attention on your college sports tour. First, let's start with the Louisiana Tech University Bulldogs and Lady Techsters. Then there's Tulane University's Green Wave. Make sure you stop at Grambling State University and watch the Tigers, and watch the other Tigers too at Louisiana State University. Finish out your tour with the Warhawks at the University of Louisiana at Monroe. I couldn't find any behind-the-scenes tours for their respective venues, so here is the contact information for each of these colleges to order game tickets:

Louisiana Tech University: https://www.latech.edu
Tulane University: https://tulanegreenwave.com
Louisiana State University: https://www.lsu.edu
University of Louisiana at Monroe: https://www.ulm.edu
Grambling State University: https://gsutigers.com

> **Did you know?** Shreveport is home to college football's Independence Bowl. It has been played in December since 1976 and is now played at Independence Stadium. For more information and tickets, visit http://independencebowl.org.

HARRAH'S LOUISIANA DOWNS

Turn the "First Call" up (the name of the starting music at a horse race) because it's that time! Take in a race at Harrah's Louisiana Downs and don't forget to place your bets on who you think the winner will be. The venue offers thoroughbred racing every May through September and quarter horse racing from January through March.

Website: https://www.caesars.com/harrahs-louisiana-downs

Contact: Harrah's Louisiana Downs, 8000 E Texas St., Bossier City LA 71111; (318) 742-5555.

DELTA DOWNS RACING

Louisiana is also home to racing at Delta Downs in Vinton. It's a few hours away from Louisiana Downs, but die-hard racing fans will be willing to make the trip.

Website: https://www.deltadowns.com

Contact: Delta Downs Racetrack Casino Hotel, 2717 Delta Downs Dr., Vinton LA 70668; (800) 589-7441.

LOUISIANA SPORTS HALL OF FAME

Louisianans love their sports, and this museum honors those who have made a name for themselves and set and broken a few records. Familiar names like Archie Manning, Willis Reed, and Shaquille O'Neal are honored as well as Audrey "Mickey" Patterson. She was the first African-American woman to win an Olympic medal in track. And that Super Bowl XLIV New Orleans Saints victory is commemorated with a signed football.

Website: https://www.louisianastatemuseum.org

Info: Louisiana Sports Hall of Fame is open Tuesday through Saturday 10:30 a.m. to 4:30 p.m. If you have special needs, please contact the museum before your arrival. Cost: adults, $5; students, seniors, and active military, $4; children 6 and under, free.

Contact: Louisiana Sports Hall of Fame, 800 Front St., Natchitoches LA 71457; (318) 357-2492.

NEW ORLEANS SAINTS / MERCEDES-BENZ SUPERDOME

I've been a Green Bay Packers fan for as long as I can remember, but when I was little I fell in love with the New Orleans Saints helmets. I don't know what it is about them, but I love them. The team has been around since 1966 and finally won the Super Bowl in 2009, their first Super Bowl appearance, just a few years after the devastating effects of Hurricane Katrina. The team plays at the Mercedes-Benz Superdome in New Orleans, which doesn't offer tours. But there is a New Orleans Saints Hall of Fame Museum, where you can see the history of the franchise. It is also home to the Sugar Bowl, college football's frequent National Championship Game (https://allstatesugarbowl.org).

Website: https://www.neworleanssaints.com

Info: The Hall of Fame Museum is open by appointment Monday through Friday 9 a.m. to 3 p.m. Cost: adults, $10; children (12 and under), seniors (ages 60 and older), and military, $5.

Contact: Mercedes-Benz Superdome, 1500 Sugar Bowl Dr., New Orleans LA 70112; (504) 587-3663.

Statue Alert!

On September 25, 2006, New Orleans Saints safety Steve Gleason blocked a punt by Atlanta Falcons punter Michael Koenen early in the first quarter of a game at the Superdome. Curtis Deloatch recovered the ball in the Falcons' end zone for a touchdown. After what was a grueling few years for the team and their community, this pivotal game-saving moment gave the residents hope. As a result, outside of the Superdome there is a statue that pays homage to Gleason. Gleason announced in 2011 that he is battling amyotrophic lateral sclerosis (ALS), otherwise known as Lou Gehrig's disease, and his journey has been documented in the film *Gleason*.

MAINE

Die-hard sports spectators won't find any professional sports teams in Maine; the state is more known for those who want to get out of the stands and participate. There is a Ski Museum in Kingfield and an Outdoor Heritage Museum. College sports fans have the University of Maine Black Bears (https://goblackbears.com) to support.

SKI MUSEUM OF MAINE

When you think of Maine, you naturally think of winter and skiing. The history of skiing is rich in this state, and this museum honors those who have made their way down the mountainside. According to the museum, their focus is "centered on educating everyone about our significant Maine ski history." You will learn how skis were made, and kids will enjoy the children's corner which exhibits skiing toys and more.

Website: www.skimuseumofmaine.org

Info: Visit the Ski Museum of Maine Wednesday through Friday 10 a.m. to 4 p.m. Free admission.

Contact: Ski Museum of Maine, 256 Main St., Kingfield ME 04947; (207) 265-2023.

MARYLAND

There are mountains, rolling hills, farmlands, beautiful waterfronts, beaches, and incredible architecture in Maryland. There are also many things for sports fans to see and do. After all, this is where the Babe was born. Talk about history!

BALTIMORE ORIOLES / ORIOLE PARK AT CAMDEN YARDS

They are now named after their state bird, but they were once in Milwaukee, Wisconsin, as one of the eight charter teams in the American League way back in 1901. They showed up in Baltimore in 1953 and have won three World Series championships—in 1966, 1970, and 1983. You can't talk about the Orioles without talking about the legendary Cal Ripken Jr., who played shortstop and third base for 21 seasons with the team. Brooks Robinson was one of the greatest third basemen in MLB history, and of course there's Hall of Fame pitcher Jim Palmer. The stadium is unbelievable, and even if you aren't an Orioles fan, it's worth a trip. Take the 90-minute tour where you can see the dugout (some tours do not allow this), press room, scoreboard control room, and more.

Website: https://www.mlb.com/orioles/ballpark

Info: Tour times are Monday through Saturday at 10 a.m., 11 a.m., noon, and 1 p.m., and Sunday at noon, 1 p.m., 2 p.m., and 3 p.m. According to the website, no tours will be held if there is a daytime game (any game that begins before 4 p.m.). When there is a 4 p.m. game, tours will be offered at 9:30 a.m., 10 a.m., 10:30 a.m., and 11 a.m. Cost: adults, $9; seniors (ages 60 and older) and children (ages 14 and under), $6; children 3 and under, free.

Contact: Oriole Park at Camden Yards, 333 W Camden St., Baltimore MD 21201; (410) 685-9800.

Good Eats

Andy Nelson played with the Baltimore Colts, but when he wasn't on the field you can guarantee he was probably BBQ-ing. Today he owns Andy Nelson's Barbeque in Cockeysville, Maryland, at 11007 York Road. Visit his website at https://andynelsonsbbq.com for more information and a menu. Don't forget the napkins!

Statue Alert!

Both Cal Ripken Jr. and Babe Ruth have statues outside of Oriole Park at Camden Yards. Make sure you get a selfie with two of the greatest the game of baseball has ever seen.

This museum in Baltimore is dedicated to the Bambino, Babe Ruth.
WIKIMEDIA COMMONS

BABE RUTH BIRTHPLACE AND MUSEUM

Two words—Babe Ruth. 'Nuff said. George Herman "Babe" Ruth Jr. was also known as the Bambino and played in the major leagues for an incredible 22 years. He started as a left-handed pitcher and became an outfielder for the New York Yankees. He set and broke many records, and at his birthplace you can learn much more about him. For example, you'll learn that he was one of the first five inducted into the Cooperstown Hall of Fame.

Website: https://baberuthmuseum.org

Info: The museum hours are April through September, Monday through Sunday 10 a.m. to 5 p.m. (7 p.m. during Orioles' home night games), and October through March, Tuesday through Sunday 10 a.m. to 5 p.m. Cost: Museum members are admitted free; adults, $10; seniors/military, $8; children (ages 5-16), $5.

Contact: Babe Ruth Birthplace and Museum, 216 Emory St., Baltimore MD 21230; (410) 727-1539.

Statue Alert!

Legendary Oriole third baseman Brooks Robinson has his own 9-foot bronze statue at 422 Eislen Street in Baltimore. The statue depicts Robinson preparing to throw out a runner at first base.

BALTIMORE RAVENS / M&T BANK STADIUM

The owner of the Cleveland Browns, Art Modell, relocated the Browns to Baltimore, but—without getting into all the specifics—wasn't allowed to take the team
name. They have won the Super Bowl twice—in 2000 and 2012. Over the years, the
Ravens have had such legends on their roster as Joe Flacco and Ray Lewis. Are you
part of the Ravens' flock?

Website: https://www.baltimoreravens.com and https://www.baltimoreravens.com/stadium

Info: There will be tours of M&T Bank Stadium, but at press time the stadium was undergoing
renovations and tour information was unavailable. Check the website for the most up-to-date info.

Contact: M&T Bank Stadium, 1101 Russell St., Baltimore MD 21230; (410) 261-RAVE (7283).

Did you know? The Baltimore Ravens Marching Band is one of only two official marching bands in
the entire NFL. What is the other team? The Washington Redskins–their marching band, founded in
1937, is the oldest.

COLLEGE SPORTS TOUR

UNIVERSITY OF MARYLAND TERRAPINS / CAPITAL ONE FIELD

Whether you are rooting for their basketball or football team, the Terrapins (known
as the Terps) have an impressive list of accomplishments. The men's basketball team
won the NCAA championship in 2002. The women accomplished the same feat
in 2006, and the football team has made multiple bowl appearances. They became
the national champions in 1951 and 1953. You're guaranteed a treat when you see
a game!

Website: https://umterps.com

Contact: Capital One Field, 90 Stadium Dr., College Park MD 20742; (301) 314-7070.

MASSACHUSETTS

It's called the "Baked Bean State," but Massachusetts is also known for its rich colonial history as home to the Freedom Trail, Bunker Hill, and other important sites related to the American Revolution. It's rich in sports history as well. After all it's home to the Red Sox, Celtics, Bruins, and the New England Patriots. The legendary Boston players include Bill Russell, Tom Brady, Ted Williams, Bobby Orr, Carl Yastrzemski, Larry Bird, and Bob Cousy. I could write page upon page on the accomplishments of each of these teams and their players.

Every April, tens of thousands of people come to the area to run the Boston Marathon, and there are just as many volunteers and spectators for the race as well. Massachusetts is also home to the Basketball Hall of Fame and the Golf Museum.

The New York/Boston rivalry is a strong one, but even this New York sports fan admits that you can't call yourself a sports fan and not put Massachusetts on your must-see list.

NEW ENGLAND PATRIOTS / GILLETTE STADIUM

Whether you love or hate the New England Patriots or love or hate their quarterback Tom Brady, it's unmistakable that they are one of the greatest teams and he is one of the greatest quarterbacks that ever played this game. Their first season was in 1960, but it was since head coach Bill Belichick and quarterback Tom Brady came along in 2000 that the Patriots have made an indelible mark on the sports record books. They have won 16 AFC East titles in 18 seasons since 2001, without having a losing season.

Want to know more about the team? You should visit the Patriots Hall of Fame (below) when you're in town for, hopefully, a game.

Website: https://www.gillettestadium.com

Contact: Gillette Stadium, One Patriot Pl., Foxborough MA 02035; (508) 543-8200.

PATRIOTS HALL OF FAME

The Patriots Hall of Fame presents touch screens, exhibits, and memorabilia of the team's history, which includes championship rings, the Vince Lombardi Super Bowl trophy, and so much more. Fans of the pigskin will love getting in the game, so to speak, including "Size-Me-Up," and a vertical jump test and reaction time test. There are rotating exhibits too, so even if you've been here before, you can come back and see something new.

Website: https://www.patriotshalloffame.com

Info: The Patriots Hall of Fame is open Monday through Friday 10 a.m. to 5 p.m., Saturday 10 a.m. to 9 p.m., and Sunday 10 a.m. to 7 p.m. Cost: adults, $10; seniors, $7; children (ages 5–12), $5; children 5 and under, free; active military and veterans free w/military ID.

Contact: Patriots Hall of Fame, 2 Patriot Pl., Foxborough MA 02035; (508) 698-4800.

BOSTON RED SOX / FENWAY PARK

The Boston Red Sox were one of the American League's eight charter franchises and are nine-time World Series champions, the last being in 2018. Their biggest rivalry is with the New York Yankees and is one of the oldest and most fierce in baseball. Let's name drop for a second—David "Big Papi" Ortiz; Carlton Fisk; Babe Ruth; Wade Boggs; Jim Rice; Cy Young; Roger Clemens; Pedro Martínez; Carl Yastrzemski—these current and future Hall of Famers played for the Red Sox at one time. You can learn more about the Red Sox and their history at Fenway Park Living Museum, which you can see when you're on the Fenway Park tour. It includes 170,000+ artifacts and 150,000+ photographs and memorabilia from Ted Williams, Ruth, and Yastrzemski among others. Don't forget that you'll see the famous "Green Monster" wall too!

Statue Alert!

Ted Williams is memorialized outside Gate B of Fenway Park.

Website: https://www.mlb.com/redsox/ballpark

Info: The one-hour tours are available 9 a.m. to 5 p.m. daily. The last stadium tour departs at 5 p.m. on non-game days and on game days the last tour departs three hours before game time. Offseason the stadium tour times are from 10 a.m. to 5 p.m. The stadium also offers shorter "Green Monster" only tours. Cost: adults, $21; children (ages 3–12), $15; military, $17.

Contact: Fenway Park, 4 Jersey St., Boston MA 02215; (877) 733-7699.

BOSTON CELTICS / TD GARDEN

The Boston Celtics have been around since the beginning of the NBA, putting their names in the record books. Fans have been entertained for years, especially by their friendly mascot, Lucky the Leprechaun. It's here at the TD Garden where such basketball legends as Larry Bird, Bob Cousy, John Havlicek, and Bill Russell have run the court. The Celtics have won the NBA championship a whopping 17 times!

The TD Garden offers behind-the-scenes tours and houses the Sports Museum.

Website: https://www.nba.com/celtics

Info: At press time, the TD Garden was undergoing construction and wouldn't be offering behind-the-scenes tours and museum tours again until summer 2020, so check the website for up-to-date information.

Contact: TD Garden, 100 Legends Way, Boston MA 02114; (617) 624-1050.

BOSTON BRUINS / TD GARDEN

One of the original six NHL franchises, the Boston Bruins are one of the oldest hockey teams in the United States. The Bruins started back in 1924, along with the Chicago Blackhawks, Detroit Red Wings, Montreal Canadiens, New York Rangers, and Toronto Maple Leafs. Speaking of six, they have won six Stanley Cup championships. The Bruins were the first NHL team to have a black player—Willie O'Ree back in 1958. The Bruins have also had such legendary players as Bobby Orr, Zdeno Chára, and Ray Bourque on their roster. They currently play in the TD Garden, which typically offers behind-the-scenes tours.

Website: https://www.nhl.com/bruins

Info: At press time, the TD Garden was undergoing construction and wouldn't be offering behind-the-scenes tours and museum tours again until summer 2020, so check the website for up-to-date information.

Contact: TD Garden, 100 Legends Way, Boston MA 02114; (617) 624-1050.

Statue Alert!

Boston Bruins legend Bobby Orr was inducted into the Hockey Hall of Fame in 1979 at age 31. Back then, he was the youngest to be inducted. Today, there is a statue in his honor outside of the TD Garden in Boston.

Cheers Bar

If you want to go where everybody knows your name, this is the place to be. In the sitcom *Cheers* bartender Sam Malone was a former pitcher for the Boston Red Sox. After his retirement, he bought the bar. *Cheers* is a real bar in Boston, with two locations (Faneuil Hall and Beacon Hill), and you should stop by at least one of them for a visit. Try the Norm challenge while you're there—nope, it's not a beer challenge, but a burger challenge, and if you finish it, they'll add your name to the wall.

Sing it with me: "Sometimes you wanna go . . ." It's the Cheers bar in Boston. WIKIMEDIA COMMONS

Website: https://cheersboston.com

Info: Children are allowed in the restaurant/bar until 10 p.m. and then afterward all patrons must be 21 and over.

Contact: Beacon Hill (the original Cheers), 84 Beacon St., Boston MA 02108; (617) 227-9605; and Faneuil Hall Marketplace, Quincy Market, South Boston MA 02109; (617) 227-0150.

COLLEGE SPORTS TOUR

BOSTON COLLEGE EAGLES / ALUMNI STADIUM

The Boston College Eagles football team was formed more than 100 years ago, in 1892. Tom Coughlin, who became head coach of the New York Giants, coached at Boston College. During his time there, he coached the Eagles to a win over Notre Dame, the first time they defeated a #1 team. Can you also say "Hail Flutie?"

Because one of the most amazing games in Eagles history took place on November 23, 1984, when Boston's quarterback, Doug Flutie, threw a last-second Hail Mary to Gerard Phelan to beat the Miami Hurricanes 47–45. Flutie passed for 472 yards and four touchdowns in that game and had a successful NFL career.

Website: https://bceagles.com

Contact: Alumni Stadium, 140 Commonwealth Ave., Chestnut Hill MA 02467; (617) 552-3000.

🏀 LISA'S PICK 🏀
NAISMITH MEMORIAL BASKETBALL HALL OF FAME

If you are a basketball fan, you're going to love the Naismith Memorial Basketball Hall of Fame in Springfield, Massachusetts. Hey, I'm not the biggest fan of watching basketball, but even I loved it!

On my trip to the area, I visited the Springfield Armory and then headed over to the Naismith, which is located in, what else, a basketball-shaped building. There are three floors and your tour starts with a photo op at the main door and an elevator that takes you to the top floor. You'll work your way down from there. The museum covers more than 40,000 square feet.

On the top floor, there are plaques and memorabilia from the Hall of Famers dating back almost 100 years. It's a lot of reading on that top floor, so plan on spending a good chunk of time if you want to see everyone. Or just look for your favorite players and read about their history and their induction.

Cool personal connection: I found players in the Hall of Fame that I have been lucky enough to interview including WNBA superstar Lisa Leslie and former Miami Heat center Alonzo Mourning.

If you are touring the Naismith with children, keep in mind that the younger ones may get a little antsy on that top floor because they probably won't know the players. You can keep their attention by showing them the easy-to-miss memorabilia that is showcased in between the plaques. I wish this stuff was taken out of the cases and put on display more at eye level. It would definitely get some attention. There are

Everyone can try to dunk at the Naismith Memorial Basketball Hall of Fame in Springfield, Massachusetts. AUTHOR PHOTO

championship rings and Olympic medals as well as oversized bronzed sneakers on display. There is a bunch of great stuff to look at if you just look down.

When you are done or if you want the kids to become a little more interested in the museum, move to the second floor where there are more interactive adventures. Check out your wingspan against Kevin Durant's or see how tall you are against a variety of pro ballers. The second floor was a lot of fun and especially great for kids. The female players and coaches are prominently featured in the exhibits—as they should be—as are the refs. (By the way, you should also check out the Women's Basketball Hall of Fame in Tennessee on page 158.)

By now, you will probably be aching to take some shots at the hoop, and the bottom floor is the perfect place because it's actually a basketball court! There is also

Website: www.hoophall.com

Info: At press time, the museum was undergoing expansion and construction. Check their website for the most up-to-date hours of operation. Cost: adults (16 and older), $25; seniors, $20; youth (ages 5–15), $16; children 4 and under, free.

Contact: Naismith Memorial Basketball Hall of Fame, 1000 Hall of Fame Ave., Springfield MA 01105; (877) 4HOOPLA.

a great gift shop and, if you are hungry, there are a few places to eat right across the hall from the Hall of Fame.

Overall, we finished everything in about an hour and a half, but you can definitely spend more time there shooting hoops and reading more than we did.

Statue Alert!

Boxers Rocky Marciano and Marvin Hagler attended Brockton High School in Brockton, Massachusetts. On their campus is the Rocky Marciano Stadium and a 30-foot-tall bronze statue of Marciano on the stadium's north end. **TRAVEL TIP:** Keep in mind that this is a high school and visitors may be questioned about their presence on campus.

Did you know? The Boston Marathon is the most elite of the marathons held across the country. If you're interested in standing on the sides rooting for your favorite runners—or want to run the race yourself—you should know that it's held every April in Boston. Visit https://www.baa.org for more information.

INTERNATIONAL VOLLEYBALL HALL OF FAME AND MUSEUM

Volleyball doesn't get nearly as much fame and attention as other sports, but this museum in Holyoke honors its history and the athletes who have put volleyball on the map. William G. Morgan invented volleyball at the Holyoke YMCA in 1895, and the museum opened in 1987. Since then, more than 100 men and women have been inducted.

Website: https://www.volleyhall.org

Info: The International Volleyball Hall of Fame and Museum is open Thursday through Sunday from noon to 4:30 p.m., year-round, or by special pre-arranged appointment. Cost: adults, $8; seniors, $5; students (ages 7–17) and active and retired military, $5; children 6 and under, free.

Contact: International Volleyball Hall of Fame, 444 Dwight St., Holyoke MA 01040; (413) 536-0926.

MICHIGAN

Michigan borders four of the Great Lakes. On top of that, it has more than 11,000 inland lakes and, of course, Detroit is the birthplace of Motown music and the automotive industry. When it comes to sports, there's so much for a fan to enjoy. The Wolverine State is home to the University of Michigan's Wolverines as well as the Michigan State Spartans. When it comes to professional sports, there are the Detroit Lions, Tigers, Red Wings, and Pistons.

> **Did you know?** The 38th president of the United States, Gerald R. Ford, grew up in Grand Rapids and was a star football player at the University of Michigan.

DETROIT LIONS / FORD FIELD

The Detroit Lions were founded in 1930, but originally were called the Portsmouth Spartans and played in Portsmouth, Ohio. It wasn't until 1934 that they moved to Detroit, and they have since won four NFL championships. Fans may not remember that though, since their last championship was in 1957 and they have never appeared in the Super Bowl. The team plays at Ford Field, which is also home to college football's Quick Lane Bowl. The stadium offers behind-the-scenes tours, which is a great way to get up-close and personal with the history of the Lions and Ford Field.

> **Website:** https://www.detroitlions.com and https://www.fordfield.com
>
> **Info:** Behind-the-scenes tour prices range from $7 to $10 per person. Ford Field offers a limited tour schedule so check the website for more information. There are also group tour packages and a package where you can take photos in the Lions locker room.
>
> **Contact:** Ford Field, 2000 Brush St., Detroit MI 48226; (313) 262-2000.

DETROIT TIGERS / COMERICA PARK

The Detroit Tigers have won four World Series championships (1935, 1945, 1968, and 1984), but there's so much more history and interesting facts about this team. Let's start with chatty Mark Fidrych, who was the 1976 American League Rookie

> **Website:** https://www.mlb.com/tigers
>
> **Info:** Public tours of Comerica last about 90 minutes and run from June to September, only on Tuesday and Friday. When games fall on Tuesday and Friday, the tours are offered at 11 a.m. and 1 p.m. Cost: adults, $5; children (ages 4–14), $5; children 4 and under, free. On non-game day Tuesdays and Fridays, tours are offered at 11 a.m., 1 p.m., and 3 p.m. Cost: adults, $6; children (ages 4–14), $4; children 4 and under, free.

of the Year. He won 19 games but was known for talking to himself on the mound. And don't forget that the legendary Ty Cobb played with the Tigers for 22 seasons.

At Comerica Park, you can take a behind-the-scenes tour of the home dugout, visiting clubhouse, visiting batting tunnel, Champions Club, media center, the Detroit Tigers Walk of Fame, and more. The Park even offers kids tours.

DETROIT RED WINGS / LITTLE CAESARS ARENA

Are you ready to go to Hockeytown? That's what fans of the Detroit Red Wings have called the area for years—it's even a Red Wings registered trademark. The Red Wings have won 11 Stanley Cup championships—the most of any franchise based in the United States. We can't talk about the Detroit Red Wings without talking about the man, Gordie Howe, who spent his first 25 years in the NHL with the Red Wings and won six Hart Trophies as the NHL's most valuable player—a hockey legend like no other. Today's Red Wings play at Little Caesars Arena, which is also home to the NBA's Detroit Pistons. The venue offers behind-the-scenes tours.

Website: https://www.nhl.com/redwings

Info: The public tour schedule for the Little Caesars Arena is limited, so check the website for more information. Cost: adults, $20; children (12 and under), seniors and military, $15.

Contact: Little Caesars Arena, 2645 Woodward Ave., Detroit MI 48201; (313) 471-3200.

DETROIT PISTONS / LITTLE CAESARS ARENA

The Pistons were born back in 1941 as the Fort Wayne (Indiana) Pistons. They moved to Detroit in 1957 and have since won three NBA championships—in 1989, 1990, and 2004. The Pistons play at Little Caesars Arena, which is also home to the NHL's Detroit Red Wings. The venue offers behind-the-scenes tours.

Website: https://www.nba.com/pistons

Info: The public tour schedule for the Little Caesars Arena is limited, so check the website for more information. Cost: adults, $20; children (ages 12 and under), seniors, and military, $15.

Contact: Little Caesars Arena, 2645 Woodward Ave., Detroit MI 48201; (313) 471-3200.

COLLEGE SPORTS TOUR

UNIVERSITY OF MICHIGAN WOLVERINES / MICHIGAN STADIUM

The 11-time national champion Michigan Wolverines have the most wins of any college football program (to date). Currently coached by former Chicago Bears quarterback Jim Harbaugh, they play their games in the "Big House," the largest stadium in the country. You can take a guided tour of Michigan Stadium and the University of Michigan's athletics campus for a fee, where you'll see the team locker room, the press box, and premium seating.

While you're here, make sure you visit the Towsley Family Museum, located inside Schembechler Hall. You will enjoy the "Win Wall" which features footballs that mark each of the program's more than 900 victories, retired jerseys, and more. Here you can also see the life-size statue of legendary coach Bo Schembechler outside the entrance to the building.

Website: https://mgoblue.com

Info: Guided tours of Michigan Stadium and the University of Michigan's athletics campus are available for a fee. The Towsley Family Museum is open Monday through Friday 9 a.m. to 4 p.m. On home game day, the museum is open two-and-a-half hours before kickoff. Free admission to the museum.

Contact: Towsley Family Museum, 1200 State St., Ann Arbor MI 48109; (734) 647-4310; Michigan Stadium, 1201 S Main St., Ann Arbor MI 48104; (734) 764-0247.

MICHIGAN STATE SPARTANS

When it comes to rivalries, the Wolverines and the Michigan State Spartans rank up there as one of the fiercest. The Michigan State basketball team made the 2018-19 Final Four, knocking out the highly favored Duke Blue Devils. The Michigan State football team has claimed six national championships (1951, 1952, 1955, 1957, 1965, and 1966). They play their football games at Spartan Stadium, while the ballers play their games at Jenison Field House. Make sure that you take your selfie with Sparty, the popular 9-foot-7 ceramic figure that weighs approximately 6,600 pounds and is a great photo op.

Website: https://msuspartans.com/facilities

Contact: Spartan Stadium, 325 W Shaw Ln., East Lansing MI; (517) 353-8147; Jenison Field House, 223 Kalamazoo St., East Lansing MI 48824; (517) 355-1610.

Statue Alert!

Speaking of Spartans, Earvin "Magic" Johnson played on the Spartans' 1979 championship team as a sophomore before he went on to an incredible professional basketball career with the Los Angeles Lakers in the NBA. Today, there is a statue of this great player at 34 Birch Road in East Lansing.

MINNESOTA

Okay here we go. This Green Bay Packers fan is required to write about Minnesota, home to one of the biggest rivals of my favorite football team—the Minnesota Vikings. Now don't get me wrong: Minnesota is a great place to visit and visitors who spend time here will enjoy the Twin Cities—Minneapolis and Saint Paul. This midwestern state was also the birthplace of the NHL's Mike Ramsey; baseball's Jack Morris; the NHL's Neal Broten; the NBA's Kevin McHale; and baseball's Dave Winfield. Now I'm not going to see the Vikings—there are some lines I won't cross—but if you want to that's cool. In addition to the Vikings, sports fans can enjoy watching the NHL's Minnesota Wild, college's Minnesota Golden Gophers, and baseball's Minnesota Twins.

MINNESOTA VIKINGS / US BANK STADIUM

Call 'em the Purple and Gold or the Purple People Eaters or just simply the Vikes, whatever you want, but you can call them exciting to watch. Although the Vikings have made multiple appearances at the Super Bowl since starting in the NFL in 1961, they have never won. I'm not going to talk about the year my Packers legend Brett Favre went over to the dark side and became a Viking for a year, but that happened. There have been many legendary players who have worn purple jerseys including Ahmad Rashad, Adrian Peterson, Randy Moss, and Fran Tarkenton. The Vikings play at US Bank Stadium, which offers 90-minute behind-the-scenes tours of the premium clubs and suites, the Thomson Reuters Press Level, stadium art collection, team locker room, stadium floor, and so much more.

Website: https://www.usbankstadium.com

Info: With the exception of blackout dates, stadium tours are offered year-round. They start on the hour with the first tour at 10 a.m. and the last tour at 4 p.m. every day except Sunday. On Sunday, the first tour is at 11 a.m. and the last tour begins at 3 p.m. Cost: adults, $19; children (ages 5-12), $7; seniors (ages 55 and older), $14; students (with valid ID), $12; active military and veterans (w/ID), $14; children 5 and under (limit 2 per accompanying adult), free.

Contact: US Bank Stadium, 401 Chicago Ave., Minneapolis MN 55415; (612) 777-8700.

MINNESOTA WILD / XCEL ENERGY CENTER

The NHL's Minnesota Wild was founded back on June 25, 1997, but it took a few years before they competed on the ice. Such incredible players as Ryan Suter, Mikko Koivu, Pierre-Marc Bouchard, and Devan Dubnyk have played for the franchise. The Wild could use some additional support here, because even though they made it to the championship in the 2002-03 season, they have yet to win a Stanley Cup.

They play at the Xcel Energy Center and behind-the-scenes public tours are offered of the stadium for groups of less than 20 people on a first-come, first-served basis.

MINNESOTA TWINS / TARGET FIELD

Back in 1924, Major League Baseball's Minnesota Twins won the World Series under the name Washington Senators. Almost 40 years later, they moved from Washington to Minnesota and won the World Series again in both 1987 and 1991 as the Twins. Over the years, such legends as Walter Johnson, Goose Goslin, Bert Blyleven, Rod Carew, and Kirby Puckett have played for the franchise. The team plays at Target Field, and if you want to explore this incredible stadium, they offer a 90-minute tour where you can see the Herb Carneal Press Box, clubhouse, dugout, suite level, Bat & Barrel, Delta SKY360 Club, Budweiser Roof Deck, and Thompson Reuters Champions Club. There's even incredible artwork to see as well as Twins memorabilia.

> **Website:** https://www.mlb.com/twins
>
> **Info:** Okay, listen closely because this gets detailed and you should look at the website before traveling to the stadium for the most up-to-date information. According to the Target Field website, from April through September, Target Stadium tours are given on non-game days Tuesday through Sunday at 11 a.m. and 2 p.m. In October, tours are given on non-game days on Friday, Saturday, and Sunday at 11 a.m. and 2 p.m. On evening game days, when the game begins at 6:10 p.m., a tour is given at 11 a.m. When the game begins at 7 p.m. or later, tours are given at 11 a.m. and 1 p.m. Game day tours may not include visits to the visitors' clubhouse, field, and dugout areas. Cost: adults, $17; seniors (ages 55 and older) and military (w/ID), $14; students (15 and older w/ID), $12; children (ages 6–14), $8; children 5 and under (limit 2 per accompanying adult), free.
>
> **Contact:** Target Field, 1 Twins Way, Minneapolis MN 55403; (612) 659-3400.

ST. PAUL SAINTS / CHS FIELD

They aren't part of Major League Baseball, but they provide a fun day at the park. Where else can you watch a team that's co-owned by comedian Bill Murray?

> **Website:** http://saintsbaseball.com
>
> **Info:** Go behind the scenes at St. Paul's CHS field with a 90-minute tour. Cost: $19 per person (non-game days) and $15 per person on game days. Visit their website for more tour information.
>
> **Contact:** St. Paul Saints–CHS Field, 360 Broadway, St. Paul MN 55101; (651) 644-6659.

MINNESOTA AMATEUR BASEBALL HALL OF FAME

Minnesota has a lot of baseball history and this Hall of Fame does a great job preserving it. Located in the St. Cloud River's Edge Convention Center on the second floor, it's open year-round. The museum has many artifacts from the minor leagues, college, high school, American Legion, and VFW, including uniforms, caps, photos, bats, balls, gloves, and programs.

Website: www.mnamateurbaseballhof.com

Info: Free admission.

Contact: St. Cloud River's Edge Convention Center, 10 4th Ave., South St. Cloud MN 56301; (800) 450-7272.

COLLEGE SPORTS TOUR

MINNESOTA GOLDEN GOPHERS

The Minnesota Golden Gophers have been playing basketball since 1905. They have won nine Big Ten championships, but only four since 1919. If you don't watch a game, you still need to check out the Williams Arena, which was originally opened in 1928 and was once called "The Barn." It's considered one of the coolest arenas in the country.

Website: https://gophersports.com

Contact: Williams Arena, 1925 University Ave., Minneapolis MN 55455; (612) 625-5000.

UNITED STATES HOCKEY HALL OF FAME

I could write a book about the unforgettable history of hockey in the United States. Hockey is fun and exciting to watch and has given us years of memorable games. Until that book gets written, the United States Hockey Hall of Fame in Eveleth, Minnesota, is a great place to visit and learn about the sport. It was dedicated in 1973 as the "National Shrine of American Hockey" and honors the players and games. You can try your own hockey skills on the replica rink, see a Zamboni in person, and watch the 1980 Olympic team as they take home the Gold (my favorite hockey match ever)!

Website: https://www.ushockeyhall.com

Info: The Hall of Fame is open Labor Day weekend through Memorial Day, Friday 10 a.m. to 5 p.m., Saturday 9 a.m. to 5 p.m., and Sunday 10 a.m. to 3 p.m. Cost: adults (ages 18 and older), $8; seniors (ages 55 and older) and juniors (ages 13–17), $7; children (ages 6–12), $6; children 6 and under, free.

Contact: United States Hockey Hall of Fame, 801 Hat Trick Ave., Eveleth MN 55734; (800) 443-7825.

A Sports Lover's Travel Story— Joe Katz

The Frozen Four is the NCAA Hockey National Championship event, which like college basketball's March Madness and Final Four, is hosted by a different city each year. We (mostly my son, nephew, and I) have attended almost every year since 2003. We've traveled to Buffalo (twice), Boston (twice), Milwaukee, Columbus, St. Louis, Denver, Washington, DC, Minneapolis/St. Paul (twice), Pittsburgh, Philadelphia, and Tampa.

We do a lot of culinary research, as we're all regional food aficionados. The site www.roadfood.com and its related books, created by the wonderful Jane and Michael Stern, are invaluable tools. They've directed us to so many great places. If the event takes place in a city with a Major League Baseball team, we usually use the off day (Friday—the tournament games take place Thursday and Saturday) to attend a ballgame, provided of course the team is in town. We've done that in Boston, Milwaukee, St. Louis, Pittsburgh, and Denver (although that got snowed out!).

The winners of four regional tournaments advance to the Frozen Four. We usually attend one of the two eastern tournaments, which are typically in a New England state. We've traveled to Providence, and Manchester in New Hampshire, Amherst and Worcester in Massachusetts, and Albany, New York, for them.

As for baseball, I've so far been to 21 current ballparks. As for the parks that are now gone, we've been to Candlestick (San Francisco), Comiskey (Chicago), Memorial (Baltimore), Turner (Atlanta), Jack Murphy (San Diego), Veterans (Philadelphia), County (Milwaukee), and of course, the dearly departed Shea Stadium.

MISSISSIPPI

Mississippi is the birthplace of The King, Elvis Presley, who might have lived in Tennessee, but was born right here in Tupelo. It's a beautifully wooded state with peaceful waters, white sandy beaches along the Gulf of Mexico, and glorious historic homes. Of course, there are plenty of sports for you to watch too. From the Ole Miss Rebels football team to the Mississippi State Bulldogs and the Southern Miss Golden Eagles, there are teams that can keep you rooting.

Then, when you want to learn more about the state's sports history, stop in and visit the Mississippi Sports Hall of Fame in Jackson.

Statue Alert!
In 2019, a statue of Rafael Palmeiro was unveiled at Mississippi State's newly renovated Dudy Noble Field. Palmeiro played for the Bulldogs before spending 20 years in MLB, starting his career at Wrigley Field with the Chicago Cubs. He hit a career 569 home runs and was one of six players to reach 3,000 hits and 500 homers.

COLLEGE SPORTS TOUR

UNIVERSITY OF MISSISSIPPI OLE MISS REBELS / VAUGHT–HEMINGWAY STADIUM

With a rebel yell, she cried . . . sorry, couldn't resist. But maybe you'll yell "more" when you see the Ole Miss Rebels play football. They were the state's first football team in 1893 and have won six Southeastern Conference titles and three national titles. They play at Vaught-Hemingway Stadium.

Website: https://olemisssports.com/

Contact: Vaught-Hemingway Stadium, All-American Dr. and Hill Dr., University MS 38677; (662) 236-1931.

MISSISSIPPI STATE BULLDOGS

Are you a member of the Bulldog Club?! It's really "ruff" not to be (see what I did there?) when you're watching the team play. Their first football season was back in 1895. Every time the team wins, listen for the cowbell! The football team plays at Davis Wade Stadium, the fourth oldest venue in all of college football behind Penn's Franklin Field, Harvard Stadium, and Georgia Tech's Bobby Dodd Stadium.

Website: https://hailstate.com

Info: Stadium tours are 45 minutes and available on Wednesday only.

Contact: Davis Wade Stadium, 90 B. S. Hood Rd., Mississippi State MS 39762; (662) 325-2323.

SOUTHERN MISS GOLDEN EAGLES

This is a cool college sports tradition—two hours prior to football game day, a cannon is fired and the ROTC, the Pride of Mississippi Marching Band, university officials, and football players march through the street to the cheers of the fans. The team, which started to play in 1912, plays at Carlisle-Faulkner Field at M. M. Roberts Stadium, which is nicknamed "The Rock at Southern Miss."

Website: https://southernmiss.com/facilities

Contact: M. M. Roberts Stadium, 118 College Dr., Hattiesburg MS 39406; (601) 266-1000.

MISSISSIPPI SPORTS HALL OF FAME AND MUSEUM

Take a self-guided tour through the Mississippi Sports Hall of Fame and Museum, where you can watch footage and interviews and explore interactive kiosks.

Website: https://msfame.com/museum

Info: The Hall of Fame and Museum is open 10 a.m. to 4 p.m., Monday through Saturday. Cost: adults (ages 18 and older), $5; seniors (ages 60 and older) and students (ages 6–17), $3.50; children age 5 and under, free; groups of 12 or more, $3 per person.

Contact: Mississippi Sports Hall of Fame and Museum, 1152 Lakeland Dr., Jackson MS 39216; (601) 982-8264.

Did you know? Jay Hanna "Dizzy" Dean, the former St. Louis Cardinals pitcher, died in 1976 and left all of his memorabilia to the Dizzy Dean Museum in Jackson. The museum has since closed and today you can find a plethora of Dean-related material at the Mississippi Sports Hall of Fame and Museum.

MISSOURI

When you think about Missouri, you probably think about grassy plains, the Ozark Mountains, and Kansas City jazz. The state also has a great sports history with the Negro Leagues and the founding of both baseball's Kansas City Royals and football's Kansas City Chiefs back in the 1960s. Over the years both teams have celebrated championships.

One of the most famous and beloved ballplayers ever, Yogi Berra, was born in St. Louis, and other famous sports Missourians include the New York Yankees' Casey Stengel and Elston Howard and Negro Leagues superstar James "Cool Papa" Bell. The PGA's Payne Stewart and boxer Michael Spinks have also called the area home.

KANSAS CITY ROYALS / KAUFFMAN STADIUM

The Kansas City Royals baseball team has won two World Series titles in 1985 and 2015 but the crown jewel here is the stadium where they play—Kauffman Stadium. Catch a game and a tour of the stadium, where you can see Outfield Plaza, the Royals Hall of Fame, the interactive Kids Area, the Royals dugout, the Crown Club, and the visitors' clubhouse. You also shouldn't miss the Kansas City Royals Hall of Fame museum. The museum includes the Clubhouse Lobby, where fans can see retired Royals numbers, the Ashwood Wall, Cooperstown Corner, The Royals Way, and other exhibits.

> **Website:** https://www.mlb.com/royals
>
> **Info:** If you have a ticket to a Royals game, you can go right into the KC Royals Hall of Fame museum. Visit the website for an extensive list of tour days/times.
>
> **Contact:** Kauffman Stadium, 1 Royal Way, Kansas City MO 64129; (816) 921-8000.

KANSAS CITY CHIEFS / ARROWHEAD STADIUM

The Chiefs have had a 50-year championship drought since they won Super Bowl III, but Kansas City loves their team nonetheless and they are still waiting for that magical day again. They were founded by Lamar Hunt, the same businessman behind the launch of Major League Soccer (MLS). The Chiefs play at Arrowhead Stadium, which offers a 90-minute behind-the-scenes guided tour that includes the press box, locker room, field, and the Chiefs Hall of Honor.

> **Website:** https://www.chiefs.com/stadium
>
> **Info:** Arrowhead Stadium tours are offered every Friday at 2 p.m. and 4 p.m. and every Saturday at 11 a.m. and 1 p.m. Tours begin at the Stadium Pro-Shop. Cost: adults, $30; children, seniors, and military, $25.
>
> **Contact:** Arrowhead Stadium, 1 Arrowhead Dr., Kansas City MO 64129; (816) 920-9300.

NEGRO LEAGUES BASEBALL MUSEUM

This museum preserves the legacy of the Negro Leagues and African-American baseball. Take a self-guided tour that features text panels, hundreds of photographs, artifacts, and several film exhibits. The tour is integrated with a timeline of baseball and African-American history.

Website: https://nlbm.com

Info: The Museum's Gallery hours are Tuesday through Saturday 9 a.m. to 6 p.m. and Sunday noon to 6 p.m. Cost: adults, $10; seniors, $9; and children (ages 5–12), $6; children 4 and under, free.

Contact: Negro Leagues Baseball Museum, 1616 E 18th St., Kansas City MO 64108; (816) 221-1920.

ST. LOUIS CARDINALS / BUSCH STADIUM

The National League's St. Louis Cardinals have won 11 World Series championships, the most behind the New York Yankees. They are also one of the oldest clubs in baseball, established in 1882. Branch Rickey established the farm system while an executive for the Cardinals, a concept later adopted by all of Major League Baseball. The legendary Cardinals who have worn the uniform and set unbelievable records include Lou Brock, Ozzie Smith, Rogers Hornsby, Dizzy Dean, Stan Musial, Bob Gibson, and Whitey Herzog.

The Cardinals' rich history is on display in a museum at Busch Stadium. The Cardinals have played at several facilities bearing the name Busch Stadium, and the Cardinals Hall of Fame showcases models of each. While you're here, you can also be one of the Cardinals' broadcasters in the booth and see all of the championship memorabilia and retired jerseys. Every Saturday home game you can see some of your favorite Cardinals alumni and get their autographs. You must have an autograph line ticket and valid museum admission to receive an autograph.

Website: https://www.mlb.com/cardinals and https://www.mlb.com/cardinals/cardinals-nation/hall-of-fame-and-museum

Info: The museum is open daily 10 a.m. to 6 p.m. The museum remains open through the seventh inning on St. Louis Cardinals' home game nights. Cost: adults, $12; children, $8; seniors or military, $10.

Contact: Busch Stadium, 700 Clark St., St., Louis MO 63102; (314) 345-9600.

Statue Alert!

Jack Buck, the Cardinals announcer from 1954 to 2001, was inducted into the Baseball Hall of Fame (see New York for more information on the Hall of Fame) in 1987. There's a statue of Buck right outside of the Cardinals' stadium.

ST. LOUIS BLUES / ENTERPRISE CENTER

You won't get the blues watching the NHL's St. Louis Blues play, but the team, which was founded in 1967, is actually named after the famous W. C. Handy song, "Saint Louis Blues." (Check it out on YouTube.) After many years of frustration, the Blues won their first Stanley Cup in 2019.

The Blues play their home games at the Enterprise Center, but as of the writing of this book the venue was undergoing renovations and not offering tours. They will bring them back, so make sure you check the website for the latest up-to-date information.

Website: https://www.nhl.com/blues and www.enterprisecenter.com

Contact: Enterprise Center (formerly Scottrade Center), 1401 Clark Ave., St Louis MO 63103; (314) 622-5400.

MISSOURI SPORTS HALL OF FAME

Numbers speak volumes and the two-story Missouri Sports Hall of Fame has them. There's 32,000 square feet of space with more than 4,000 items of sports memorabilia and exhibits. If you're a fan of racing there's a NASCAR simulator you can try. How about throwing the pigskin around or trying to hit against a Major League Baseball pitcher? This interactive museum is fun for all ages.

And there are statue alerts all over the place. There are numerous busts and statues of famous Missouri athletes and coaches.

Website: http://mosportshalloffame.com

Info: The museum is open Monday through Saturday 10 a.m. to 4 p.m., and Sunday noon to 4 p.m. Cost: adults, $5; children (ages 6–15) and students, $3; seniors (ages 55 and older), $4; family of 4, $14; groups of 10 or more, $2/person; children 5 and under, free.

Contact: Missouri Sports Hall of Fame, 3861 E Stan Musial Dr., Springfield, MO 65809; (417) 889-3100.

THE COLLEGE BASKETBALL EXPERIENCE

Whether you're past college age, not old enough for college yet, or fall somewhere in between, The College Basketball Experience is just plain fun. Here you can even call one from the ESPN-U desk, all while learning about the sport.

Website: https://collegebasketballexperience.com

Info: The College Basketball Experience is open Monday through Saturday 10 a.m. to 6 p.m. and Sunday 11 a.m. to 6 p.m. May be closed Monday and Tuesday at certain times of year: call ahead. Cost: adults, $15; children (ages 4–17), $12; seniors and military, $11; children 3 and under, free.

Contact: The College Basketball Experience, 1401 Grand Blvd., Kansas City MO 64106; (816) 949-7500.

COLLEGE SPORTS TOUR

UNIVERSITY OF MISSOURI TIGERS / MEMORIAL STADIUM

Roar! The University of Missouri Tigers started playing football in 1890 and have won a host of college championships and bowl games since. If numbers impress you, there are 33 bowl game appearances, including 10 majors: four Orange Bowls, three Cotton Bowls, two Sugar Bowls, and one Fiesta Bowl; 15 conference titles, five division titles, and two national championships. The football team plays at Faurot Field at Memorial Stadium in Columbia.

If college hoops are more your thing, the Tigers men's basketball team plays at Mizzou Arena and was a charter member of the Big 12 Conference.

Website: https://mutigers.com

Contact: Faurot Field at Memorial Stadium, Columbia MO 65203; (573) 882-6501. No tours of Faurot Field/Memorial Stadium. For Mizzou Arena, you can request a tour at https://mutigers.com/documents/2017/2/22/17_tour_request_form.pdf?id=9420 at least 30 days in advance, but filling out the form does not guarantee a tour. Prearranged 30-minute tours are Monday through Thursday 9 a.m. to 3 p.m. and are not available on game days or university holidays.

MISSOURI STATE UNIVERSITY BEARS / JQH ARENA

More college sports hoops are on the agenda, so get your tickets to see the Missouri State Bears basketball team. They play at the JQH Arena in Springfield.

Website: https://jqharena.missouristate.edu

Contact: JQH Arena, 685 S John Q. Hammons Pkwy., Springfield MO 65897; (417) 836-3300.

MONTANA

No matter what the season, Montana is beautiful—the mountains and the parks will take your breath away. So come and stay awhile, enjoy what Mother Nature has to offer, and then take in a few college sports games as well.

COLLEGE SPORTS TOUR

UNIVERSITY OF MONTANA GRIZZLIES / WASHINGTON–GRIZZLY STADIUM

Call them the "Griz" and enjoy a football game at Washington–Grizzly Stadium in Missoula. The Grizzlies hold records for most playoff appearances in a row (17), Big Sky Conference titles in a row (12), and overall playoff appearances (19). Their biggest rivalry is with the Montana State University Bobcats.

Website: https://gogriz.com

Contact: Washington–Grizzly Stadium, 32 Campus Dr., Missoula MT 59812; (406) 243-4749.

MONTANA STATE UNIVERSITY BOBCATS / BOBCAT STADIUM

And in this corner, the Montana State Bobcats, who started in 1897 and have won three national championships (1956, 1976, and 1984) since. They compete against the Grizzlies every year in the Brawl of the Wild. They play in the aptly named Bobcat Stadium in Bozeman.

Website: https://msubobcats.com

Contact: Bobcat Stadium, 1 Bobcat Cir., Bozeman MT 59718; (406) 994-4221.

NEBRASKA

Nebraska is known for its prairies and dunes. It's called the "Cornhusker State," so why not see a Cornhuskers game?

> **Did you know?** In 1950, Omaha became the home of the annual College World Series. If you want to go, visit http://cwsomaha.com for more information.

COLLEGE SPORTS TOUR

UNIVERSITY OF NEBRASKA–LINCOLN CORNHUSKERS / MEMORIAL STADIUM

The Nebraska Cornhuskers are one of the few football programs to win 800 or more games, and they've won five national championships: 1970, 1971, 1994, 1995, and 1997. They haven't won a national championship since, but they are a fun team to watch play. They play their games at Memorial Stadium in Lincoln. The stadium actually has an NCAA-record streak of consecutive sellouts dating back to 1962, so good luck snagging a ticket!

> **Website:** www.huskers.com/ViewArticle.dbml?DB_OEM_ID=100&ATCLID=208126061
>
> **Contact:** Memorial Stadium, One Memorial Stadium, 800 Stadium Dr., Lincoln NE 68588; (402) 472-4224.

NEVADA

Nevada isn't just Las Vegas, but it's definitely the draw of the state. The good news for sports fans is that there is plenty to see in between hitting the slot machines or watching one of the fabulous shows on the strip. The NFL approved the move of the Oakland Raiders to the city, which will take place in 2020, while the WNBA introduced the Las Vegas Aces in 2018, who currently play at Mandalay Bay (https://aces.wnba.com).

VEGAS GOLDEN KNIGHTS / T-MOBILE ARENA

They are the newest team to hit the ice in the National Hockey League and, to be honest, they are my favorite hockey team. During their first year, I caught a game of theirs on television and was immediately hooked. I could say it was their game play, but my love for them started before the game even began. The Vegas Golden Knights brought the Las Vegas showmanship and theater to the ice, where we could see the Knight mascot "attack" someone playing the other team's mascot as part of their pregame hype. Of course the Knight always wins. (According to the internet, some people loved this and became fans too, while others were adamant that the team should just stick to playing hockey. Give me a break. If it brought new fans to the sport, why not?)

It was so cool and drew me in, so I watched the game and then the next and the next. They continued on to do something that not many teams do their first season—they went to the Stanley Cup Finals! They didn't win, much to my sadness, and they finished third in their division the next season, but they won me over. I will go see a game just because of that original excitement. You should too. Because what happens in Vegas on the ice deserves to be shared with every sports fan.

Website: https://www.nhl.com/goldenknights and www.t-mobilearena.com/plan-your-visit/arena-tours

Info: Don't just watch a game. Take a one-hour behind-the-scenes tour of the T-Mobile Arena where the Knights play. You'll see the luxury suites, Hyde Lounge, press area, video control room, Zamboni room, dressing rooms, and visiting team locker rooms. Dates and times vary so check out the website for more information. Cost: Starting at $25 per person. Take note that children 4 years and younger are not permitted on the tour.

Contact: T-Mobile Arena, 3780 S Las Vegas Blvd., Las Vegas NV 89158; (702) 692-1600.

COLLEGE SPORTS TOUR

UNIVERSITY OF NEVADA, LAS VEGAS / SAM BOYD STADIUM

Las Vegas isn't all about glitz, glamour, and adult entertainment. It's about college sports too, and the University of Nevada, Las Vegas, has that covered. Go ahead and yell for the Rebels! (The Rebel yell, get it?) For the 2020 season the Rebels will move from Sam Boyd Stadium to Allegiant Stadium, a 65,000-seat domed stadium in Paradise.

Website: https://unlvrebels.com and www.allegiantstadium.com

Contact: Sam Boyd Stadium, 7000 E Russell Rd., Las Vegas NV 89122; (702) 895-3761.

UNIVERSITY OF NEVADA WOLF PACK / LAWLOR EVENTS CENTER

The University of Nevada Wolf Pack men's basketball team has appeared in the NCAA Division I tournament nine times. Maybe the year you go to a game it will be 10! They play their games at the Lawlor Events Center in Reno.

Website: https://www.unr.edu/lawlor/venue-information

Contact: Lawlor Events Center, 1500 N Virginia St., Reno NV 89557; (775) 784-4444.

Good Eats

Looking for a great place to watch the game? Las Vegas has a bunch of them. Try the TAP Sports Bar on the MGM Grand casino floor next to Hakkasan. It has 60 HDTVs, and then there's Lagasse's Stadium at The Palazzo.

WEBSITES: https://mgmgrand.mgmresorts.com/en/restaurants/tap-sports-bar.html and https://www.venetian.com/towers/the-palazzo.html

NEW HAMPSHIRE

New Hampshire is small-town beauty, noted for its beautiful fall foliage, pristine lakes, and mountainous landscapes. Not too much going on here in terms of sports—no pro teams per se, although I've always said you should support minor-league teams because you never know who you'll see that will become the next big thing. New Hampshire is home to the New Hampshire Fisher Cats, a Double-A affiliate of MLB's Toronto Blue Jays, and the Manchester Monarchs, the ECHL affiliate of the NHL's LA Kings. There are also a few stops you can make on your college sports tour, and racing fans will want to visit during the summer to enjoy the Monster Energy NASCAR Cup Series at the New Hampshire Motor Speedway.

NEW HAMPSHIRE MOTOR SPEEDWAY / NORTH EAST MOTOR SPORTS MUSEUM

Every summer, New Hampshire is filled with NASCAR fans who are here to watch the races each weekend in July. If you can't make it in July, visit in September when the Speedway hosts a variety of NASCAR races then too, including the NASCAR Whelen Modified Tour Musket 250 and the NASCAR K&N Pro Series East global race. While you're there, make sure you visit the North East Motor Sports Museum, located right at the south entry to the Speedway.

At the 10,000 square foot museum, you'll get a close-up view of motorcycles, drag cars, trophies, and more racing memorabilia. There's a 25-foot-long trophy case and an extensive library of racing magazines. NASCAR's own Joey Logano is a New Hampshire native and proudly honored at the museum.

Websites: https://www.nhms.com and https://www.nemsmuseum.com

Info: Check the track for times and dates of races and ticket prices. The museum is open Friday, Saturday, and Sunday 10 a.m. to 4 p.m. during the summer with limited hours in the winter. There are extended days and hours during NHMS race weekends. Cost: general admission, $10; seniors , $7; children 12 and under, free.

Contact: Museum: 922 NH-106, Loudon NH 03307; (603) 783-0183. Racetrack: 1122 Route 106 North, Loudon, NH 03307; (603) 783-4931.

NEW ENGLAND SKI MUSEUM

Bode Miller, a former World Cup alpine ski racer and Olympic and World Championship gold medalist, was born in Easton, New Hampshire, and you can learn a lot about his amazing career at the New England Ski Museum. The museum now has two locations—one in Franconia and the other in North Conway. The two locations have different exhibits covering skiing history.

Website: http://newenglandskimuseum.org

Info: The Franconia Notch Museum is open 10 a.m. to 5 p.m. all week long, from Memorial Day through the end of ski season at Cannon Mountain, which is normally in early April. Admission is free.

Contact: Franconia location: 135 Tramway Dr., Franconia, NH 03580; (603) 823-7177; North Conway location: 2628 White Mountain Hwy., North Conway NH 03860; (603) 730-5044.

COLLEGE SPORTS TOUR

UNIVERSITY OF NEW HAMPSHIRE WILDCATS / WILDCAT STADIUM

Become a Wildcat for a day when you take in a game and root on a team that established its roots back in 1893. Maybe you will score tickets to a game with one of their rivals, the Dartmouth Big Green (see below).

Website: https://unhwildcats.com

Contact: Wildcat Stadium, 155 Main St., Durham NH 03824; (603) 862-4000.

DARTMOUTH COLLEGE BIG GREEN / MEMORIAL FIELD

The Big Green Ivy League football team has won only one national championship—way back in 1925—since their humble beginnings in 1881, but they have since won 25 conference championships. While you're in the area, try to catch a game between Dartmouth and the University of New Hampshire Wildcats and watch a rivalry in action.

Website: https://dartmouthsports.com

Contact: Memorial Field, 4 Crosby St., Hanover NH 03755; (603) 646-1110.

NEW JERSEY

When it comes to sports and sports entertainment in New Jersey, your travel card is definitely full. Here's the funny thing though, and don't let it confuse you. If you're a die-hard sports fan, you probably already know that there are some New York sports teams that play in New Jersey, but still keep the New York name. So if you're looking for the New York Giants, you've been directed here because they play at MetLife Stadium in East Rutherford, New Jersey.

NEW YORK RED BULLS / RED BULL ARENA

This Major League Soccer team got its start in 1996 as the New York/New Jersey MetroStars and started playing at Giant Stadium, but have since settled in on their name and location. Yes, they are owned by the company that owns the famous drink.

The last time they were in the MLS Cup finals was in 2008, but oh boy are they still exciting to watch! They offer many fan experiences, including the opportunities for kids of all ages to be on the field with the players, so check out their website for more information way in advance of your visit.

Website: https://www.newyorkredbulls.com

Contact: Red Bull Arena, 600 Cape May St., Harrison NJ 07029; (973) 268-8420.

YOGI BERRA MUSEUM AND LEARNING CENTER

Some of my favorite Yogi Berra-isms: "It ain't over till it's over." "When you come to a fork in the road, take it." "If you don't know where you are going, you'll end up someplace else." Seriously folks, as silly as some of the things were that he said, Yogi Berra is truly one of the most beloved baseball players to ever play the sport. At this interactive museum, you'll learn about Yogi's incredible career as a 10-time World Series champion who was also a recipient of the Presidential Medal of Freedom, our nation's highest civilian honor. It's a learning center too, and the museum changes some of the exhibits so check the website for up-to-date information.

Website: https://yogiberramuseum.org

Info: The museum is open Wednesday through Sunday noon to 5 p.m. . Cost: adults, $10; children (ages 18 and under) and seniors, $5; veterans and Montclair State students free.

Contact: It's located on the campus of Montclair State University, 8 Yogi Berra Dr., Little Falls NJ 07424; (973) 655-2378.

UNITED STATES GOLF ASSOCIATION MUSEUM

Whether you love to watch or love to play, this museum is for any golf fan. The United States Golf Association museum has golf artifacts, including documents, books, videos, and documentaries. You can learn about the history of the game and relive some of its greatest moments.

> **Website:** www.usga.org
>
> **Info:** The Museum is open to visitors from Tuesday through Sunday 10 a.m. to 5 p.m., and is closed on Monday and major holidays. Cost: adults, $10; seniors, $7; USGA members, $5; children (ages 13–17), $3.50; children 12 and under, free.
>
> **Contact:** United States Golf Association Museum, 77 Liberty Corner Rd., Liberty Corner NJ 07938; (908) 234-2300.

NEW YORK GIANTS / METLIFE STADIUM

Giant blue! The New York Giants were founded in 1925 and have four NFL championships (pre–1970 AFL-NFL merger) and four Super Bowl championships, with the latest in 2011. Such MVPs as Frank Gifford, Y. A. Tittle, and Lawrence Taylor have donned the uniform. They play—along with the New York Jets, who share the venue—at MetLife Stadium. You can schedule a behind-the-scenes tour of this incredible venue where you will see the Commissioners Club, press box, and luxury suites, and get to go on the field!

> **Website:** https://www.giants.com and https://www.metlifestadium.com
>
> **Info:** Tour schedules can be a little complicated. They are offered on Saturday, but are limited when there are concerts, etc., so I refer you to the website for the best scheduling information. Cost: adults (ages 13 and older), $17; children (ages 5–12) and seniors, $12; children 4 and under, free.
>
> **Contact:** MetLife Stadium, 1 MetLife Stadium Dr., East Rutherford NJ 07073; (201) 559-1515.

NEW YORK JETS / METLIFE STADIUM

J-E-T-S, Jets, Jets, Jets! If you're a New Yorker, you either love/hate the New York Giants or love/hate the Jets. You don't love both. The New York Jets were established in 1960, but were the New York Titans until 1963. They won Super Bowl III in 1969, thanks to quarterback "Broadway" Joe Namath, when they beat the Baltimore Colts. The New York Jets play—along with the New York Giants, who share the venue—at MetLife Stadium. You can schedule a behind-the-scenes tour of this incredible facility where you will see the Commissioners Club, press box, and luxury suites, and get to go on the field!

Website: https://www.newyorkjets.com and https://www.metlifestadium.com.

Info: Tour schedules can be a little complicated. They are offered on Saturday, but are limited when there are concerts, etc., so I refer you to the website for the best scheduling information. Cost: adults (ages 13 and older), $17; children (ages 5–12) and seniors, $12; children 4 and under, free.

Contact: MetLife Stadium, 1 MetLife Stadium Dr., East Rutherford NJ 07073; (201) 559-1515.

NEW JERSEY DEVILS / PRUDENTIAL CENTER

The New Jersey Devils have had a lot of name changes throughout their lifetime, which started in 1974. They were first the Kansas City Scouts in Kansas City, Missouri. Then they became the Colorado Rockies and in 1982 moved to New Jersey and became the Devils. They have won the Stanley Cup three times (1994-95, 1999-2000, 2002-03). The Devils play at the Prudential Center in Newark.

Website: https://www.nhl.com/devils and https://www.prucenter.com

Contact: Prudential Center, 25 Lafayette St. Newark NJ 07102; (973) 757-6000.

COLLEGE SPORTS TOUR

FAIRLEIGH DICKINSON KNIGHTS / ROTHMAN CENTER

There isn't anything as exciting as watching college basketball, so if you're in the New Jersey area during hoops season, stop in and watch the Fairleigh Dickinson Knights play.

Website: https://fduknights.com

Contact: Fairleigh Dickinson University, Rothman Center, 1000 River Rd., Teaneck NJ 07601; (201) 692-2208.

PRINCETON UNIVERSITY TIGERS / POWERS FIELD

The Princeton Tigers played Rutgers University back in 1869 in what many believe was the first American football game. Today, this Ivy League school still remains a thrill to watch.

Website: www.princetontigersfootball.com

Contact: Powers Field, 21 Jadwin Gym, Princeton NJ 08544; (609) 258-3514.

RUTGERS UNIVERSITY SCARLET KNIGHTS / SHI STADIUM

That first football game I mentioned under Princeton against this team, the Scarlet Knights? Well, the Scarlet Knights are said to have won 6–4 (isn't that a baseball score?). Rutgers is said to be "the birthplace of college football" so it's a don't-miss on your college sports tour.

Website: https://www.rutgers.edu/athletics

Contact: SHI Stadium, 1 Scarlet Knight Way, Piscataway NJ 08854; (732) 445-5100.

SETON HALL UNIVERSITY PIRATES / PRUDENTIAL CENTER

The Pirates play at the Prudential Center in Newark, New Jersey.

Website: https://shupirates.com/ and https://www.prucenter.com

Contact: Prudential Center, 25 Lafayette St., Newark NJ 07102; (973) 757-6000.

NEW MEXICO

New Mexico was prominently featured in the television series *Breaking Bad* (my fave) over the last few years, but it's not all they are known for. Its topography is stunning and New Mexicans experience more than 300 days of sunshine each year, which means that it's easy to have a smile on your face when you're visiting, especially if you're a college sports fan.

COLLEGE SPORTS TOUR

UNIVERSITY OF NEW MEXICO LOBOS / DREAMSTYLE STADIUM

The New Mexico Lobos men's basketball team began in 1899 and started competing in 1920. They've been Mountain West Conference champs multiple times and have made it to the Sweet 16 twice. They have been playing at Branch Field at Dreamstyle Stadium since 1960.

> **Website:** https://golobos.com
>
> **Contact:** Dreamstyle Stadium, 1414 University Blvd. SE, Albuquerque NM 87106; (505) 925-5626.

NEW MEXICO STATE UNIVERSITY AGGIES / AGGIE MEMORIAL STADIUM

If you're going to fill out your college sports card, make sure you take a trip to see the Aggies play.

> **Website:** https://nmstatesports.com
>
> **Contact:** New Mexico State, 1810 E University Ave., Las Cruces NM 88003; (575) 646-1420.

NEW MEXICO BOWL GAME

If you love college football, then seeing a bowl game is a must on your sports travel to-do list. In New Mexico, the New Mexico Bowl Game is a biggie. It's played in Albuquerque each year, so check out the website when you travel to see who's playing.

> **Website:** https://newmexicobowl.com
>
> **Contact:** New Mexico Bowl Game, 801 University SE, Suite 104, Albuquerque NM 87106; (505) 925-5999.

NEW YORK

Start spreadin' the news! It's my home state—I was born and raised as a New Yorker and, when it comes to sports, we don't fool around. We are home to the Mets, Yankees, Bills, Knicks, Nets, Islanders, Sabres, and Rangers, as well as great horse racing and museums that celebrate all different kind of sports, including bare knuckle boxing! I could go on forever about The Big Apple, but how about we just get to what you should be seeing and doing.

BARE KNUCKLE BOXING HALL OF FAME

There are many types of fighting sports—gloved boxing, MMA, and, of course, bare knuckle boxing, and this hall of fame has a great history behind it. It includes the training barns used by famous bare knuckle boxer John L. Sullivan to prepare for the last Bare Knuckle Boxing Championship of the World against Jake Kilrain. That match went a whopping 75 rounds in 1889. The barns were untouched for more than 120 years until they were saved in 2009. You can tour these barns and see the wrestling room and Sullivan's original training equipment, as well as the "Room of Repose" where Sullivan and his trainer William Muldoon rested together.

Website: https://www.bareknuckleboxinghalloffame.com

Info: Set up your tour by sending the Hall of Fame an email using the form on the website, or contact them at the number below.

Contact: Bare Knuckle Boxing Hall of Fame, 5 Hughes St., Belfast NY 14711; (585) 610-3326.

INTERNATIONAL BOXING HALL OF FAME

Speaking of boxing, here's another museum that honors the sport and the boxers who have made it famous, including the one and only Muhammad Ali. The museum opened in 1989. A year later the first class of boxing legends, including Muhammad

Website: www.ibhof.com

Info: The International Boxing Hall of Fame is open Monday through Friday 9 a.m. to 5 p.m. and Saturday and Sunday 10 a.m. to 4 p.m. Cost: adults, $13.50; seniors, $11.50; youth (ages 7–15); $8.50; children 6 and under, free.

Contact: International Boxing Hall of Fame, 360 North Peterboro St., Canastota NY 13032; (315) 697-7095.

Don't get knocked out when you see the Boxing Hall of Fame in Canastota, New York. WIKIMEDIA COMMONS

Ali, came to the museum to see themselves honored. The Hall of Fame holds an annual induction ceremony in early June as the highlight of a four-day celebration of boxing and its legends, so try to time your visit to that time.

JACKIE ROBINSON MUSEUM

The Jackie Robinson Foundation received a gift of more than $6 million a few years ago, which allowed them to start construction on the museum that honors this baseball legend. In an article written by Mark Newman of MLB.com, Sharon Robinson, Jackie's daughter, was quoted as saying, "The Jackie Robinson Museum is important because it's my mom's last big thing that she wanted to achieve."

Jackie Robinson was 28 years old when he broke into the major leagues, and he won the unified Rookie of the Year Award. He led the National League in stolen bases, was named to his first All-Star Game, and helped the Brooklyn Dodgers win the pennant. Major League Baseball chose his number as the first one to ever retire for every team. The museum will house Robinson's memorabilia, tell the story of his career, and offer films and educational programming. It is said it will be "a place for vibrant dialogue on critical social issues."

Website: www.jackierobinson.org

Info: As of this writing, the museum wasn't open yet, so make sure to check the website for the most up-to-date information.

Contact: Jackie Robinson Museum, One Hudson Square, 75 Varick St., 2nd Floor, New York NY 10013; (212) 290-8600.

The Lake Placid Winter Olympics Museum in Lake Placid, New York, is dedicated to amateur sports and memorable Olympic experiences. WIKIMEDIA COMMONS

LAKE PLACID WINTER OLYMPIC MUSEUM

The Winter Olympics happen every four years and often leave us with some great memories. Do you remember the "Miracle on Ice" when the US hockey team beat the Russians? Located in the Olympic Center, the Museum is only a few feet from the arena where the 1980 victory took place— now named after that team's coach, Herb Brooks. You'll also see the first indoor Winter Olympic skating arena and learn more about winter sports in Lake Placid from artifacts, photographs, and videos. At the Olympic Center athletes continue to train and compete every day, so you never know what future Olympic medalist you're going to see!

Website: www.lpom.org

Info: The museum is open daily from 10 a.m. to 5 p.m. It is closed Ironman Sunday (which is July 26 in 2020), Thanksgiving, and Christmas. Cost: Free with the Olympic Sites Passport (https://www.whiteface.com/plan/olympic-sites-passport). If purchased separately: adults and teens, $7; juniors (ages 12 and under) and seniors, $5; children 6 and under, free.

Contact: Olympic Center, 2634 Main St., Lake Placid NY 12946; (518) 302-5326.

HARNESS RACING MUSEUM AND HALL OF FAME

New York has a great history with horse racing, especially harness racing, and this museum in the Hudson Valley town of Goshen is where you can see the sleighs of Currier & Ives, horse sculptures, and more. Make sure to tour the beautiful Hudson Valley while you're here.

Website: https://www.harnessmuseum.com

Info: Museum galleries and the gift shop are open Tuesday through Sunday 10 a.m. to 4 p.m. The museum is closed on Monday. Free admission.

Contact: Harness Racing Museum and Hall of Fame, 240 Main St., Goshen NY 10924; (845) 294-6330.

SARATOGA RACE COURSE

New York State is a great place to vacation, from New York City to the upstate farms and every place in between. If you're looking for a quaint city to spend your summers, look no further than Saratoga Springs, located just south of Lake George and home to the exciting Saratoga Race Course.

From the end of July through each Labor Day, you can take in an exciting day at the Saratoga Race Course and enjoy traditional seating with clubhouse admission. If you're into a little gambling action now and then besides the horses, stay at the Saratoga Casino Hotel where you can try your hand at more than 1,700 slots and electronic table games while enjoying live racing.

Keep in mind that the racing schedule makes Saratoga a popular vacation spot in the summer and lodging can be difficult to find at peak racing times. Take the 45-minute walking tour of the 150 years of race course history too! Find out why they ring a bell at 17 minutes to post and why there is a canoe in the lake in the infield.

Website: https://www.nyra.com/saratoga

Info: Tours are scheduled at 9:30 a.m., 10:30 a.m., 11:30 a.m., 12:30 p.m., 1:30 p.m., and 2:30 p.m. each racing day. Cost: $3 per person or $10 for a family.

Contact: Saratoga Race Course, 267 Union Ave., Saratoga Springs NY 12866; (518) 584-6200.

☞ LISA'S PICK ☜
THE ADELPHI HOTEL

Stay at the Adelphi Hotel, located in the heart of downtown Saratoga Springs at 365 Broadway. For more information, visit adelphi-hospitality.com.

ROME SPORTS HALL OF FAME AND MUSEUM

When in Rome, stop by and see the Rome Sports Hall of Fame and Museum. Here you can see memorabilia from NASCAR champions, speed boat champions, bowlers, and Olympians. There are also 120 plaques featuring those who have been inducted.

Website: www.when-in-rome.com/romesportshalloffameandmuseum

Info: Rome Sports Hall of Fame and Museum is open from Memorial Day to Labor Day, Wednesday through Saturday 10 a.m. to 5 p.m. and Sunday noon to 5 p.m. Closed Monday and Tuesday.

Contact: Rome Sports Hall of Fame and Museum, 5790 Rome–New London Rd., Rome NY 13440; (315) 339-9038.

NATIONAL MUSEUM OF RACING AND HALL OF FAME

To learn more about racing history, make sure to take a side trip to this museum in Saratoga before or after your visit to the track. Here you'll see art, artifacts, and memorabilia about thoroughbred racing through the years.

Website: https://www.racingmuseum.org

Info: Memorial Day through Labor Day, open every day 9 a.m. to 5 p.m. From the day after Labor Day through New Year's Eve, the museum is typically open Wednesday through Sunday, 9 a.m. to 5 p.m. (closed Monday and Tuesday). Cost: adults, $10; students and senior citizens (ages 55 and older), $5; children 5 and under, free.

Contact: National Museum of Racing and Hall of Fame, 191 Union Ave., Saratoga Springs NY 12866; (800) JOCKEY4.

EMPIRE CITY CASINO / YONKERS RACEWAY

I grew up with Yonkers Raceway practically in my backyard. I was born and raised in Yonkers and I've not only gone to the County Fair there, but I also watched what the Raceway is known for—harness racing. So much fun! The Raceway was founded in 1899 as Empire City Trotting Club (from 1907 to 1943) and the one and only Seabiscuit is just one of many famous thoroughbreds to race at the track. Here's a fun sports tidbit too—in 1972, Yonkers Raceway was acquired by Tim Rooney, the son of Steelers founder Art Rooney. A few years ago, the Raceway also added the Empire City Casino, which now has more than 5,000 slots and electronic gaming tables, making it the sixth largest casino floor in the nation, including Las Vegas and Indian casinos.

Website: https://www.empirecitycasino.com/racing

Info: The casino is open from 10 a.m. to 6 a.m. Check the website for racing schedules.

Contact: Yonkers Raceway, 810 Yonkers Ave., Yonkers NY 10704; (914) 968-4200.

BELMONT PARK RACE COURSE

It's one of the best race courses out there, and if you're going to tour all of the racetracks, you have to include this on your list. Located in Elmont, New York, this elite 450-acre track is home to the Belmont Stakes held on the first or second Saturday every June.

Website: https://www.nyra.com/belmont

Contact: Belmont Park Race Course, 2150 Hempstead Turnpike, Elmont NY 11003; (718) 641-4700.

LISA'S PICK
NATIONAL BASEBALL HALL OF FAME AND MUSEUM

If you love baseball, history, or a combination of both, you have to travel to Cooperstown, New York. When I was a little girl, my mother told me that we went to Cooperstown, but I don't remember it. I love baseball and, as a New York Mets fan, I promised myself that I would "return" to Cooperstown—after all I only live a few hours away—and visit it again, but this time I would remember it. So I went, and the truth is, I'll never forget it.

Cooperstown is a quaint little community known for its baseball legacy and as home of the historic Doubleday Field and the National Baseball Hall of Fame, a museum that is visited by more than 300,000 people each year. But there's so much more to Cooperstown! Baseball first though: Spring training was still underway when I went, but that is considered offseason for the area and, as a result, the museum wasn't that busy at all.

This really worked out well for Ej "The Rainmaker" Garr and I when we visited the museum together. Ej has an emotional connection to baseball, especially to Joe DiMaggio, and watching him visit the museum for the first time ever was just as fun as experiencing it myself.

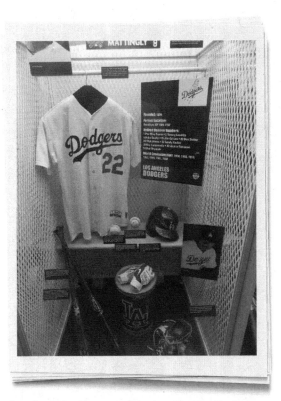

See the retired jerseys of the Los Angeles Dodgers and other teams at the National Baseball Hall of Fame in Cooperstown, New York. AUTHOR PHOTO

Without too many tourists around, I had time to stop and read the historic plaques about what the players contributed to the game and absorb the history of it all without being elbow to elbow with other fans. Honestly though, you can spend *hours* at the museum and still not have time to read all of the plaques and see all the displays they have. There are a few downsides to coming in the offseason though. First, the hours to the museum are shortened and many of the small shops in town are closed for the season. Because we were on a short stay, there is so much that we wanted to see that we couldn't. Coming at the right time of year for the Hall of Fame Classic or the induction ceremonies will give your trip that complete baseball ambiance—but plan ahead if you are visiting then and be ready for big crowds.

We wished we could have been there during those special times, but the trip was still pretty awesome. To think that so many legendary baseball players—such as Joe DiMaggio, Babe Ruth, Cy Young, and Jackie Robinson—walked where I walked was an incredible feeling. For me, the most emotional part was a door marked "Colored Entrance," which took my breath away, and reading about the struggles that black athletes had in the game. However, it was also pretty awesome to see the museum also honor women of baseball and the fans who make the game memorable.

As for where you should stay, we were invited to stay at the Inn at Cooperstown as guests of the owners Sherrie and Marc Kingsley, who bought the place years ago. It really was like staying at a home away from home. Honestly, it was also my first experience staying at either an inn or bed-and-breakfast, and I'm likely to do it again. It was a very cozy and very clean experience and except for a few creaky hallway stairs, the place was pretty quiet.

Your trip wouldn't be complete without a visit to the Baseball Wax Museum, Cooperstown Bat Company, and a meal at Doubleday's I. We ate a late dinner at Doubleday's and I had a burrito. Yummy! Cooperstown is a great trip to take, whether you are the baseball fan or you have kids who love the sport.

Women in Baseball are represented at the National Baseball Hall of Fame and Museum in Cooperstown, New York, and deservedly so. Author Photo

NATIONAL BASEBALL HALL OF FAME AND MUSEUM

Website: https://baseballhall.org

Info: Cost: adults (ages 13–64), $25; seniors, $25, but a $5 senior discount is automatically applied at checkout w/valid photo ID; juniors (ages 7–12), $15; children 6 and under free with paid adult.

Contact: National Baseball Hall of Fame and Museum, 25 Main St., Cooperstown NY 13326; (888) HALL-OF-FAME.

THE INN AT COOPERSTOWN

Website: https://www.innatcooperstown.com

Contact: The Inn at Cooperstown, 16 Chestnut St., Cooperstown NY 13326; (607) 547-5756.

HEROES OF BASEBALL WAX MUSEUM

Website: https://www.thisiscooperstown.com/attractions/heroes-baseball-wax-museum

Info: Season is March to December.

Contact: Baseball Wax Museum, 99 Main St., Cooperstown NY 13326; (607) 547-1273.

COOPERSTOWN BAT FACTORY

Website: https://www.cooperstownbat.com/store-factory-hours

Info: Cooperstown Bat Company factory hours are Monday through Friday 9 a.m. to noon and 1 p.m. to 3 p.m. Closed Saturday and Sunday. You can see a free bat turning demonstration during operating hours.

Contact: Cooperstown Bat Company Factory, 3152 County Highway 11, Hartwick NY 13348; (888) 547-2415.

DOUBLEDAY I

Website: https://www.facebook.com/DoubledayCafe

Info: Open daily, full menu 7 a.m. to 11 p.m., bar only after 11 p.m.

Contact: Doubleday I, 93 W Main St., Cooperstown NY 13326; (607) 547-5468.

NEW YORK METS / CITI FIELD

Sing along with me! "MEET THE METS, MEET THE METS, Step right up and greet the Mets! Bring your kiddies, bring your wife; Guaranteed to have the time of your life!" (There's more to the song, but that will get you started!)

If you haven't read it yet, you should go and read the introduction to this book, where you will learn about the love I have for this team. Ever since I was a little girl, I've been watching the New York Mets no matter how the season has gone (no jokes please). When I like a team I stick with them. If you want to see such current Mets as Jacob deGrom, Noah Syndergaard, or Brandon Nimmo, then come and see a game. Now remember, this is not Shea Stadium. Shea Stadium was the legendary venue where the New York Mets played for 45 seasons, but it closed back in 2008.

You can take a non–game day tour of Citi Field and see the Jackie Robinson Rotunda, production control room, press box, the warning track, press conference room, Mets Hall of Fame and Museum, and more.

Website: https://www.mlb.com/mets/ballpark/tours

Info: The one-hour tours are given on Wednesday and Friday, beginning at 11 a.m. Cost: adults, $20; children (ages 12 and under), $15. The Hall of Fame and Museum is open during all home games and all fans with a ticket to the game have access. However, the Mets Hall of Fame and Museum is *not* open on non–game days. Access on non–game days is only available via a Citi Field tour.

Contact: Citi Field, 23-01 Roosevelt Ave., Queens NY 11368; (718) 507-8499.

Did you know? George Herman "Babe" Ruth is buried in the Gate of Heaven Cemetery in Hawthorne, only 30 miles from Yankee Stadium. Many baseball fans make a pilgrimage to the headstone every year.

Website: www.gateofheavenny.com

NEW YORK YANKEES / YANKEE STADIUM

Oh, if you were only able to visit the original Yankee Stadium! The legends who walked that field, the memories that happened there. It literally brings tears to my eyes just thinking about it. I have to tell you though, the new Yankee Stadium is so worth the visit. It's beautiful and you're still standing on treasured ground. After all, the New York Yankees have won 27 World Series championships and, love 'em or hate 'em, watching a game here is special. Even as a Mets fan, I rooted on our fellow New York team (my other half is a Yankees fan) when they made it to the playoffs, but my team didn't. I went to a playoff game and the energy was exhilarating.

A baseball autographed by the legendary slugger Joe DiMaggio can be seen at the museum at Yankee Stadium. AUTHOR PHOTO

Lisa Iannucci and Ej Garr pose in front of photos of Babe Ruth and Lou Gehrig at Yankee Stadium. AUTHOR PHOTO

Roger Maris and Mickey Mantle jerseys at the Yankee Stadium Museum in the Bronx. Author Photo

You can tour the stadium on both non–game days and game days (with a ticket to the game, of course). On the classic, non–game day tour, you can see the New York Yankees Museum, Monument Park, the press box, and/or the dugout. Monument Park is behind the outfield fence and consists of plaques of the many legends who have worn the Yankee pinstripes.

Website: https://www.mlb.com/yankees

Info: The times of the Classic Tours are 11 a.m., 11:20 a.m., 11:40 a.m., noon, 12:20 p.m., 12:40 p.m., 1 p.m. 1:20 p.m., and 1:40 p.m. They also offer a bilingual tour at 1 p.m. There are no Classic Tours on game days when the game starts at 1:10 or 4:05. If you are touring on a game day, the times that the tours are offered are plentiful, so check the website for more information. Check out my tips about visiting Yankee Stadium for more information on what you'll see and experience.

Contact: Yankee Stadium, One E 161st St., Bronx NY 10451; (212) YANKEES.

New York Yankees Travel Tips

1. If you live in proximity to the Metro North train station or are traveling from New York City while on vacation to see the game, the convenience of the 153rd Street stop completely trumps driving to the park. We got on the train in our Hudson Valley hometown and got off right at the park. A short walk on the pathway over and we were there. No parking hassles at all. Totally worth it.

2. Speaking of the pathway, take your time and *look down* while you walk into the stadium. You will see historic markers along the pathway that tell you a little about the history of the team. It's easy to miss these, but they are pretty cool.

3. Don't believe that you can't see a Yankees game without breaking your budget. Our tickets were $40 apiece (yes, we were up pretty high), but you can find bleacher seats for $25. If you're looking for tickets on specialty days or playoff games, they will be much more expensive. The train (from our stop) cost us $26 each roundtrip, so if you live in or are vacationing in the New York City area add in whatever it is where you are. I bought a footlong hot dog for $7 and a soda for $6.25 (souvenir cup). If you have small children or want to split the footlong and soda with a friend, you can save more money. Of course if you're going to throw in a few beers, your budget might get a little strained. Try to eat lunch before you go to the park and maybe just grab a snack or two.

4. That being said, I absolutely hate the seats. I had nowhere to stretch my legs and I have a bad knee. After about an hour sitting there, I had to get up and walk. A few more inches in front of me would've been much more comfortable.

5. If you have a ticket to the game, a visit to the museum (included in your ticket price) is a must. Take a half inning off and go see it, whether or not you're a Yankees fan.

Yankee Stadium before the crowds arrive for a home game Author Photo

BROOKLYN NETS / BARCLAYS CENTER

While the Nets have won some division titles, they have yet to secure an NBA championship. Their franchise was established in 1967 as part of the American Basketball Association (ABA). They have had some name changes along the way—first as the New Jersey Americans, then the New York Nets, then the New Jersey Nets, and finally, in the summer of 2012, the Brooklyn Nets.

Website: https://www.nba.com/nets and https://www.barclayscenter.com/teams/detail/brooklyn-nets

Contact: Barclays Center, 620 Atlantic Ave., Brooklyn NY 11217; (917) 618-6100.

NEW YORK KNICKS / MADISON SQUARE GARDEN

The New York Knicks, or Knickerbockers as they are more formally known, were established back in 1946. They won NBA championships in 1970 and 1973 and have had such legendary players as Patrick Ewing, Walt Frazier, Earl "The Pearl" Monroe, and Bob McAdoo on their roster.

They play at a legendary venue, Madison Square Garden (MSG)—and so do the New York Rangers—and you can go behind the scenes here on a tour that includes state-of-the-art virtual reality technology. The Garden was built back in the 1960s and has an incredible sports and entertainment history.

Website: https://www.msg.com/madison-square-garden and https://www.nba.com/knicks

Info: Tours of MSG run daily from 9:30 a.m. to 3 p.m. and 12:15 p.m. to 3 p.m. on Knicks game days. Tours depart every half hour and last approximately 75 minutes. Player locker rooms are subject to availability and are not accessible on game days. Cost: adults, $35; Children (ages 12 and under), students (w/valid ID), and seniors, $30.

Contact: Madison Square Garden, 4 Pennsylvania Plaza (7th Avenue between W 31st and W 33rd Streets). New York NY 10001; (212) 465-6741.

NEW YORK CITY FC (NYCFC) / YANKEE STADIUM

We went to Yankee Stadium and a soccer game broke out. What? Well it's true. Right now (as of this printing) the NYCFC is playing at Yankee Stadium, but there are talks to create a soccer-specific stadium for NYCFC in the future, so check the website for up-to-date information. In the meantime, here is the Yankee Stadium information. Make sure you take in an MLS game while you're here. The team has been around since 2015 and is extremely popular.

Website: https://www.mlb.com/yankees and https://www.nycfc.com

Info: The times of the Classic Tours are 11 a.m., 11:20 a.m., 11:40 a.m., noon, 12:20 p.m., 12:40 p.m., 1 p.m. 1:20 p.m., and 1:40 p.m. They also offer a bilingual tour at 1 p.m. There are no Classic Tours on game days when the game starts at 1:10 or 4:05. If you are touring on a game day, the times that the tours are offered are plentiful, so check the website for more information. Check out my article about visiting Yankee Stadium for more information on what you'll see and experience.

Contact: Yankee Stadium, One E 161st St., Bronx NY 10451; (212) YANKEES.

NEW YORK RANGERS / MADISON SQUARE GARDEN

I firmly admit that out of all the sports, hockey was my least favorite until "The Rainmaker" came along. My older brother tried to get me to like hockey—he was a die-hard New York Islanders fan—but it didn't work. It wasn't until I actually found myself wearing a Rangers jersey, rooting for them in the playoffs while Ej was downing a plate of wings, that I realized how much fun hockey could be (I still root for the Rangers, but am now a Vegas Knights Fan—see the Nevada section for more on that).

The Rangers history is exciting and extensive, so I'm just going to say if you find yourself in New York City, go see a game. They are one of the Original Six, along with the Boston Bruins, Chicago Blackhawks, Detroit Red Wings, Montreal Canadiens, and Toronto Maple Leafs, to compete in the NHL until the league's expansion in 1967. Today, you might just catch their unbelievable goaltender Henrik Lundqvist in action, and if you do, lucky you!

Website: https://www.msg.com/madison-square-garden and https://www.nhl.com/rangers

Info: Tours of MSG run daily from 9:30 a.m. to 3 p.m. and 12:15 p.m. to 3 p.m. on Knicks days. Tours depart every half hour and last approximately 75 minutes. Player locker rooms are subject to availability and are not accessible on game days. Cost: adults, $33; children (ages 12 and under), students (w/valid ID), and seniors, $28.

Contact: Madison Square Garden, 4 Pennsylvania Plaza (7th Avenue between W 31st and W 33rd Streets), New York NY 10001; (212) 465-6741.

NEW YORK ISLANDERS / NASSAU COLISEUM

The second of three professional hockey teams in New York, the New York Islanders were founded in 1972 and won four consecutive Stanley Cups between 1980 and 1983. Today, the Islanders split their home games between the Barclays Center and Nassau Coliseum until their new arena near Belmont Park is opened in 2021.

Website: https://www.nhl.com/islanders

Contact: Barclays Center, 620 Atlantic Ave., Brooklyn NY 11217; (917) 618-6100.

BUFFALO SABRES / KEYBANK CENTER

Last, but not least, rounding out the three New York professional hockey teams is the Buffalo Sabres. When you are watching a game, be sure to do the Sabre Dance!

Unfortunately the Buffalo Sabres haven't won a Stanley Cup championship yet, but the team advanced to the Stanley Cup Finals in 1975—losing to the Philadelphia Flyers—and in 1999 when they lost to the Dallas Stars. Maybe the year you see a game will be their lucky one! They play their games at KeyBank Center in Buffalo.

Website: https://www.nhl.com/sabres

Contact: KeyBank Center, 1 Seymour H Knox III Plaza, Buffalo NY 14203; (716) 855-4100.

BUFFALO BILLS / NEW ERA FIELD

The Buffalo Bills are one of three New York professional football teams, along with the New York Giants and the New York Jets, but they are the only New York team to actually play in New York. They play in New Era Field in Buffalo. Unfortunately, the Buffalo Bills struggle a bit and haven't won a Super Bowl, but seeing any professional team play live is fun and the Bills are no exception. New Era Field offers a behind-the-scenes tour. You'll see the press areas, luxury clubs and suites, the field, and much more.

Website: https://www.buffalobills.com

Info: Stadium tours are available on select Fridays, May through October. You can book a stadium tour by using the My One Buffalo mobile app. Cost: $15 per person.

Contact: New Era Field, 1 Bills Dr., Orchard Park NY 14127; (716) 648-1800.

COLLEGE SPORTS TOUR

SYRACUSE UNIVERSITY ORANGE / CARRIER DOME

Whether you're there to watch Syracuse's football team or Jim Boeheim's basketball team, there's no doubt that the Orange are fun to watch. There have been many legends who have played here, including Ernie Davis, Jim Brown, and Floyd Little. The amazing Carrier Dome is a must-see on your trip to the area.

Website: https://cuse.com

Info: No formal Carrier Dome tours, but you can peek if you're in the area. You might see the national championship trophy that the Syracuse basketball team won in 2003 or the Heisman Trophy that was awarded to Ernie Davis in 1961—he was the first African American who won the award. No cost to peek.

Contact: Carrier Dome, 900 Irving Ave., Syracuse NY 13244; (315) 443-2121.

ST. JOHN'S UNIVERSITY RED STORM / MADISON SQUARE GARDEN

At the time of writing this book, the St. John's University Red Storm basketball team had 1,900 total wins, putting them at #6 on the list of teams with the most victories in NCAA Division I men's college basketball. Doesn't that make you want to see a game? If you do, the men's team plays their games at Madison Square Garden, so tour the facility while you're there.

Website: https://www.msg.com/madison-square-garden and https://redstormsports.com

Info: Tours of MSG run daily from 9:30 a.m. to 3 p.m. and 12:15 p.m. to 3 p.m. on Knicks days. Tours depart every half hour and last approximately 75 minutes. Player locker rooms are subject to availability and are not accessible on game days. Cost: adults, $33; children (ages 12 and under), students (w/valid ID), and seniors, $28.

Contact: Madison Square Garden, 4 Pennsylvania Plaza (7th Avenue between W 31st and W 33rd Streets), New York NY 10001; (212) 465-6741.

FORDHAM UNIVERSITY RAMS / JACK COFFEY FIELD

Down in "Da Bronx" you'll find the Fordham University Rams, and you should definitely try to watch the basketball or football teams, depending on when you're traveling. The Rams football team plays their games at Jack Coffey Field, which also served as the venue for the 2016 US Open Cup in soccer when the New York Cosmos played against the NYCFC.

Website: https://fordhamsports.com

Contact: Jack Coffey Field, 441 E Fordham Rd., Bronx NY 10458; (718) 817-1000.

NORTH CAROLINA

Welcome to the Tar Heel State! North Carolina is known for many things, including the success of the Wright Brothers, who launched us off the ground and into the air, and the Great Smoky Mountains. When it comes to sports, it's a close call as to which is bigger—college sports or NASCAR. While you debate that, here's a list of things to do.

COLLEGE SPORTS TOUR

UNIVERSITY OF NORTH CAROLINA TAR HEELS / DEAN SMITH CENTER

The North Carolina Tar Heels men's basketball program won seven NCAA men's college national championships between 1924 and 2017. Tar Heel alumni who went on to legendary basketball careers include Michael Jordan, James Worthy, and Billy Cunningham. The Tar Heels play at the Dean Smith Center.

Website: https://goheels.com

Info: There are no tours of the Dean Smith Center, but you can visit the second and third floors during regular business hours. You should call ahead of time though to make sure that the building is open on the days you are visiting.

Contact: Dean E. Smith Center, 300 Skipper Bowles Dr., Chapel Hill NC 27514; (919) 962-2296.

CAROLINA BASKETBALL MUSEUM

Want to know more about the Tar Heels and their basketball history? Make a stop at the Carolina Basketball Museum, which is right on the UNC campus on the first floor of the Ernie Williamson Athletics Center. You'll see tributes to Tar Heels legends including Dean Smith, Michael Jordan, and Roy Williams. There are artifacts, videos, photos, and interactive exhibits for you to enjoy.

Website: https://goheels.com/news/2017/6/26/general-carolina-basketball-museum

Info: The museum is open to the general public Monday through Friday from 10 a.m. to 4 p.m. and Saturday from 9 a.m. to 1 p.m. Admission is free.

Contact: Carolina Basketball Museum, 450 Skipper Bowles Dr., Chapel Hill NC 27514; (919) 962-6000.

NORTH CAROLINA STATE WOLFPACK

It's so cool talking about a football team when the start of their program—like many colleges—begins in the 1800s. In this case, it's 1892. The Wolfpack are great to watch and deserve a cheer or two during the game. They play at Carter-Finley Stadium and you just might say it's one of the best you've visited on your college sports tour!

Website: https://gopack.com

Contact: Carter-Finley Stadium, 4600 Trinity Rd., Raleigh NC 27607; (919) 834-4000.

DUKE UNIVERSITY BLUE DEVILS

Watching the Duke Blue Devils men's basketball team play is a treat! Coached by the legendary Mike Krzyzewski, Duke has won five NCAA championships but their stats go on and on from there. Just get to a game! If you read my introduction to this book, you'll see that the team brings excitement all of the time.

While you're there make sure you visit the Duke Basketball Museum, which celebrates the heritage and success of the basketball program. You'll see trophies, videos, and memorabilia. You can also peek at the Duke Athletics Hall of Fame which has portraits of its members.

Website: www.goduke.com

Info: The Duke Basketball Museum and Sports Hall of Fame are open 9 a.m. to 5 p.m. weekdays, with weekend hours around home football and basketball games. The area is free of charge for all visitors.

Contact: Cameron Indoor Stadium, 115 Whitford Dr., Durham NC 27705; (919) 684-8111. Duke Basketball Museum and Sports Hall of Fame, 306 Towerview Dr., Schwartz-Butters Athletic Center, Durham NC 27708; (919) 613-7500.

WAKE FOREST UNIVERSITY DEMON DEACONS / BB&T FIELD

Complete your North Carolina College Sports Tour with the Wake Forest University Demon Deacons. Their football team plays at BB&T Field. Lawrence Joel Veterans Memorial Stadium—adjacent to the Dixie Classic Fairgrounds—is home to Wake Forest men's and women's basketball.

Website: https://godeacs.com

Contact: BB&T Field, 499 Deacon Blvd., Winston-Salem NC 27105; (336) 758-3322; Lawrence Joel Veterans Memorial Stadium, 2825 University Pkwy., Winston-Salem NC 27105; (336) 758-2410.

CAROLINA PANTHERS / BANK OF AMERICA STADIUM

The NFL's Carolina Panthers really do belong to the Carolinas—they play in Charlotte, North Carolina, and their training camp is located at Wofford College in Spartanburg, South Carolina. Their first NFL season was 1995, and in 1996 they made it to the NFC championship before losing to my Packers—er, the Green Bay Packers, who won the Super Bowl that year.

The Panthers reached the Super Bowl again following the 2015 season, but lost to the Denver Broncos. Make sure you take a behind-the-scenes tour of Bank of America Stadium, but remember it won't be on game day so you have to plan accordingly.

Website: https://www.panthers.com

Info: Bank of America Stadium public tours are offered most Wednesdays at 10 a.m. and Fridays at 10 a.m. and noon year-round. Cost: adult, $6; seniors (ages 55 and older) and military, $5; children (ages 5-17), $4; children 5 and under, free. The tour typically lasts approximately 75 minutes. It's important to note that the stadium tours are fully accessible, but wheelchairs are not provided. No tours on game days.

Contact: Bank of America Stadium, 800 S Mint St., Charlotte NC 28202; (704) 358-7000.

CAROLINA HURRICANES / PNC ARENA

Batten down the hatches, here come the Hurricanes! This NHL team started out as the New England Whalers and came into the NHL in 1979 as the Hartford Whalers. The team came to North Carolina in 1997 and nine years later won the 2006 Stanley Cup over the Edmonton Oilers in seven games. The Hurricanes play at the PNC Arena.

Website: https://www.nhl.com/hurricanes and https://www.pncarena.com

Contact: 1400 Edwards Mill Rd., Raleigh NC 27607; (919) 467-7825.

CHARLOTTE HORNETS / SPECTRUM CENTER

I'm not a fan of hornets in general, but I'm a basketball fan and these NBA Charlotte Hornets are okay with me. Partially owned by the legendary b-baller himself, Michael Jordan, the Hornets came into the league in 1988 as an expansion team and were once called the New Orleans Hornets. They haven't won an NBA championship yet, but, hey, they might be "buzzing" around one soon, who knows. (See what I did there?)

The Hornets play in the Spectrum Center.

Website: https://www.nba.com/hornets and www.spectrumcentercharlotte.com

Info: A tour of the Spectrum Center can be scheduled by calling (704) 688-8128.

Contact: Spectrum Center, 333 E Trade St., Charlotte NC 28202; (704) 688-8600.

NORTH CAROLINA SPORTS HALL OF FAME

Want to learn more about North Carolina's sports history? The North Carolina Sports Hall of Fame is located on the third floor of the North Carolina Museum of History in downtown Raleigh.

Contact: 5 East Edenton St., Raleigh NC 27601; (919) 807-7900.

Info: The Sports Hall of Fame is open Monday through Saturday 9 a.m. to 5 p.m. and Sunday noon to 5 p.m. Admission is free.

Website: https://www.ncshof.org/thehall

NASCAR HALL OF FAME

This is your sport. This is your house, and this is your NASCAR Hall of Fame in Charlotte. You'll find a theater, simulated racetracks, a Hall of Horror, even a Pit Stop Cafe for you to enjoy. Did you know that you can even go to induction weekend if you plan your trip right? A new class of five inductees will be named once a year. You never know who you'll see that year!

Website: www.nascarhall.com

Info: The NASCAR Hall of Fame is open Monday 10 a.m. to 5 p.m. and Wednesday through Sunday 10 a.m. to 5 p.m. Cost: adults, $25; seniors, $22; military, $18; children (ages 3–7, $12; youth (ages 8–12), $18.

Contact: NASCAR Hall of Fame, 400 E M.L.K. Jr. Blvd., Charlotte NC 28202; (704) 654-4400.

NORTH CAROLINA BASEBALL MUSEUM

If you can't get to Cooperstown, New York, for the holy grail of baseball museums, or even if you can, this museum is a little taste of what's to come. Located at the minor-league Fleming Stadium, you'll see cases upon cases of memorabilia and information about baseball players who were from North Carolina, including Enos Slaughter, Catfish Hunter, and Gaylord Perry. In another room, you'll see memorabilia about collegiate and minor leagues.

Website: http://ncbaseballmuseum.com

Info: The museum is open Thursday through Saturday 10 a.m. to 4 p.m. and Sunday 1 p.m. to 5 p.m. Free admission (donations accepted).

Contact: North Carolina Baseball Museum, 300 Stadium St., Wilson NC 27893; (252) 296-3048.

RICHARD PETTY DRIVING EXPERIENCE

Just imagine getting behind the wheel of a car and pretending to be Richard Petty or any legendary NASCAR driver. The Richard Petty Driving Experience provides NASCAR experiences from riding along in a car for a few laps to a session where you are the one behind the wheel. Costs vary so visit the website. The company is based out of North Carolina, but the sessions are also offered at Daytona International Speedway in Florida and Talladega Superspeedway in Alabama.

Website: https://www.drivepetty.com

Contact: Richard Petty Driving Experience, 6025 Victory Ln., Concord NC 28027; (704) 886-2400.

NORTH DAKOTA

The beauty that is North Dakota is hard to put into words. Sometimes you can just drive for miles looking at the farmland and the fields. Some people might find that boring, but not me. I think untouched land is stunning. Theodore Roosevelt lived here, but more importantly to sports fans, so did Roger Maris. There's a museum in his honor too.

Forget shopping at the West Acres Mall in Fargo and visit the Roger Maris Museum instead. WIKIMEDIA COMMONS

ROGER MARIS MUSEUM

A Roger Maris museum at a mall? Yes, you read that right. In 1961, the New York Yankees' Roger Maris hit a record 61 home runs, breaking Babe Ruth's single-season record of 60 home runs set in 1927. He didn't want a museum, but then decided

Website: https://westacres.com/attractions/roger-maris-museum

Info: The mall is open Monday through Saturday 10 a.m. to 9 p.m. and Sunday noon to 6 p.m. Cost: free, but donations welcome.

Contact: Roger Maris Museum, West Acres, 3902 13th Ave. South, Suite 3717, Fargo ND 58103; (800) 783-6450.

that it would be okay as long as it was somewhere people would see it and it was free. It makes sense now that the museum is located at West Acres in Fargo, where the legend was born. Here you can see a replica of Maris's locker, and displays and artifacts from his entire career.

COLLEGE SPORTS TOUR

NORTH DAKOTA STATE BISON / FARGODOME
Do you hear that? It's the Thundering Herd, otherwise known as the North Dakota State Bison. You should stop by and see a game at the Fargodome if you're in the area.

Website: https://fightinghawks.com

Contact: Fargodome, 1800 N University Dr., Fargo ND 58102; (701) 241-9100.

OHIO

Seven US presidents were born in the Buckeye State—Ulysses S. Grant, Rutherford B. Hayes, James A. Garfield, Benjamin Harrison, William McKinley, William H. Taft, and Warren G. Harding. When it comes to sports history, it is also responsible for the first major-league baseball team—the Cincinnati Red Stockings. You'll find plenty to see and do in this sports-obsessed state.

CINCINNATI REDS / GREAT AMERICAN BALL PARK

The Cincinnati Reds have won five World Series titles since they hit the field as the Cincinnati Red Stockings in 1882. The Big Red Machine, as they are called, has included such baseball greats as Johnny Bench, Pete Rose, Dave Concepción, Ken Griffey Sr., and others who have left their mark on the game and set records. The Reds play at the Great American Ball Park, and if you're here for a game, you must take a tour of the stadium and the Cincinnati Reds Hall of Fame and Museum (see below). Take in all the history of this amazing team.

On the regular non–game day, 90-minute behind-the-scenes tour, you'll see Crosley Terrace, Kroger Fan Zone, the press box, the warning track behind home plate, the dugouts, and more. The Reds also introduced a 50-minute home game day tour as well where fans can see the warning track behind home plate and in front of the dugouts, the Budweiser Bowtie Bar area, the Kroger Fan Zone, and more.

Website: https://www.mlb.com/reds

Info: The tour schedule gets a little complicated when you add in non–game day and game day tours, so just check out the website for more information. Cost: adults, $22; seniors (ages 60 and older) and students (ages 13-18 or college w/ID), $17; children (ages 5-12) and military (active/veteran w/ID), $10.

Contact: Great American Ball Park, 100 Joe Nuxhall Way, Cincinnati OH 45202; (513) 381-7337.

CINCINNATI REDS HALL OF FAME AND MUSEUM

The Cincinnati Reds Hall of Fame and Museum is a 16,000-square-foot facility with exhibit galleries located on two floors. Visit the website for game day and non–game day schedules.

Website: https://www.mlb.com/reds/hall-of-fame

Info: Cost: adults, $12; seniors (ages 60 and older) and students (ages 13-18 or college w/ID), $8; children 12 and under and active military/veterans w/ID free.

Contact: Cincinnati Reds Hall of Fame and Museum, 100 Joe Nuxhall Way, Cincinnati OH 45202; (513) 381-7337.

CLEVELAND INDIANS / PROGRESSIVE FIELD

Also from Ohio, the Cleveland Indians came into the major leagues in 1887 and have won two World Series championships since—the latest was in 1948. That's a long time! While you're there, look for John Adams—and no, this isn't a reference to our Founding Father. Cleveland icon John Adams is a drummer who has been pounding a bass drum at almost every Cleveland Indians home game since 1973.

The Indians play at Progressive Field, which holds behind-the-scenes stadium tours. On select days you get to see the batting cages and the visitors' clubhouse, as well as the dugout and other areas.

Website: https://www.mlb.com/indians

Info: Public walk-up tours are rain or shine, are about 60 minutes in length, and run from May 1 to August 31. Cost: adults (ages 15 and older), $15; seniors (ages 60 and older), $12; children (ages 14 and under), $12. Visit the website for more information.

Contact: Progressive Field, 2401 Ontario St., Cleveland OH 44115; (216) 420-4487.

Did you know? Abbott and Costello aren't just known for their funny "Who's on First" routine. Check out their skit on Bob Feller and Enos Slaughter. (You can find it on YouTube.com.) Feller was known as "The Heater from Van Meter," "Bullet Bob," and "Rapid Robert," and played for 18 seasons with the Cleveland Indians.

BASEBALL HERITAGE MUSEUM

Want to know more about Bob Feller, Satchel Paige, and other famous Cleveland Indians ballplayers? Or just about baseball in general? Then add the Baseball Heritage Museum onto your must-see list while you're here. Here you will be able to peruse photographs, letters, programs, uniforms, and other incredible baseball memorabilia. The museum is located in the former ticket office at historic League Park.

Website: http://baseballheritagemuseum.org

Info: Baseball season hours are Wednesday and Friday 1 p.m. to 5 p.m., Saturday 10 a.m. to 4 p.m., and Sunday noon to 4 p.m. Admission is free, although donations are welcome.

Contact: Baseball Heritage Museum, 6601 Lexington Ave., Cleveland OH 44103; (216) 789-1083.

CLEVELAND BROWNS / FIRSTENERGY STADIUM

See a game and be part of the Cleveland Browns Dawg Pound! You'll be in great company because there have been some famous fans of this NFL team, including the one and only Elvis Presley; the WWE's Jerry "The King" Lawler, The Miz, and Dolph Ziggler; and country superstar Brad Paisley. The team hasn't been to the playoffs in a long time and has never been to the Super Bowl, but when you're in Cleveland, do what Clevelanders do and that's root!

Website: https://www.clevelandbrowns.com and http://firstenergystadium.com

Contact: FirstEnergy Stadium, 100 Alfred Lerner Way, Cleveland OH 44114; (440) 891-5001.

Statue Alert!

Statues at FirstEnergy Stadium honor former owner Al Lerner, all-time great running back Jim Brown, and Hall of Fame quarterback Otto Graham.

CINCINNATI BENGALS / PAUL BROWN STADIUM

The 1960s were all about freedom, hippies, love, and the founding of the Cincinnati Bengals, who came into the American Football League in 1966. Their head coach was Paul Brown, who led the Bengals until 1975. Today the Bengals play their games at Paul Brown Stadium. The Bengals haven't won a Super Bowl yet, but they made it to the playoffs as recently as 2015.

While you're there, maybe do the "Ickey Shuffle" in honor of Elbert L. "Ickey" Woods, a fullback who played his entire NFL career with the Cincinnati Bengals and did his famous touchdown dance in the end zone.

Website: www.bengals.com/

Info: You can schedule Paul Brown Stadium tours by calling (513) 621-3550. Tours are held Monday through Friday 10 a.m. to 2 p.m. from April 1 through mid-July. Cost: Adults, $11; children (ages 18 and under) and seniors, $9. To schedule a tour please call (513) 455-4800.

Contact: Paul Brown Stadium, One Paul Brown Stadium, Cincinnati OH 45202; (513) 621-3550.

CLEVELAND CAVALIERS / ROCKET MORTGAGE FIELDHOUSE

LeBron James spent many years playing for the Cleveland Cavaliers. The Cavs debuted in 1970 and won their first NBA championship in 2016. They play in Rocket Mortgage FieldHouse.

Website: https://www.nba.com/cavaliers

Contact: Rocket Mortgage FieldHouse, 1 Center Court, Cleveland OH 44115; (888) 894-9424.

PRO FOOTBALL HALL OF FAME

From its early days to today's superstars and record-setting athletes, the Pro Football Hall of Fame is a must-see for anyone who likes the pigskin either as a fan or a player. It will take about three or four hours to get through it all, but it's so worth it. In the (kind of) words of Dr. Seuss, "Oh the places you go and the stuff you see!"

Website: https://www.profootballhof.com

Info: The museum is open in the winter, spring, and fall, from 9 a.m. to 5 p.m. Summer hours (Memorial Day through Labor Day) are 9 a.m. to 8 p.m. Cost: adults (ages 13–64), $26; seniors, $22; children (ages 6–12), $19; children 6 and under, free. You can take a personal tour of the Hall of Fame as well. Cost: non-members, $10 per person. The one-hour tours are offered every day at 11 a.m.

Contact: Pro Football Hall of Fame, 2121 George Halas Dr. NW, Canton OH 44708; (330) 456-8207.

FC CINCINNATI / WEST END STADIUM

Say hello to one of the newest teams in Major League Soccer. The Cincinnati FC played their inaugural season in 2019. Right now the team plays at Nippert Stadium, an outdoor stadium on the campus of the University of Cincinnati. Their permanent home will be West End Stadium, when it's done being built—it is scheduled to be finished in 2021. If you have the opportunity to watch a game there, take a good look at the state-of-the-art, $250+ million soccer stadium that was built in the West End neighborhood of Cincinnati just for the team.

Website: https://www.fccincinnati.com

Contact: Nippert Stadium, 2700 Bearcat Way, Cincinnati OH 45221; (513) 556-2287.

COLLEGE SPORTS TOUR

OHIO STATE BUCKEYES / OHIO STADIUM

Next to the New York Yankees and Boston Red Sox, the Ohio State Buckeyes and Michigan Wolverines may have the biggest rivalry in the country. This adrenaline-filled competition is the last football game on the fall schedule, alternating venues, and it is very difficult to snag a ticket. The Buckeyes play at Ohio Stadium, more commonly known as "The Shoe," the fourth-largest on-campus facility in the nation. Take a behind-the-scenes tour of this incredible stadium, and get the Buckeye experience and walk the sidelines where coach Woody Hayes once roamed. You'll see the collegiate press box and visit the Steinbrenner Band Center, home to the "Best Damn Band in the Land."

Website: https://ohiostatebuckeyes.com

Info: A two-week notice is required to schedule a tour of Ohio Stadium, but you cannot schedule tours more than six months in advance, so plan accordingly. Tours are available Monday through Friday 9 a.m. to 4:30 p.m. and last for about an hour and a half. Cost: groups of 10 or fewer, $100.

Contact: Ohio Stadium, 411 Woody Hayes Dr., Columbus OH 43210; (614) 292-6330.

OHIO STATE BUCKEYES / VALUE CITY ARENA, SCHOTTENSTEIN CENTER

The rivalry between Michigan and Ohio State is just as competitive in basketball, so if you want to see this hoops competition, get tickets to a game at Value City Arena. In case you were wondering, the Buckeyes are leading the series 97–77 as of 2019.

Website: https://ohiostatebuckeyes.com and https://www.schottensteincenter.com

Info: Tours of the Schottenstein Center typically last about 1 to 1.25 hours. Call for cost information. No tours during football season.

Contact: Schottenstein Center, 555 Borror Dr., Columbus OH 43210; (614) 688-3939.

OHIO UNIVERSITY BOBCATS / PEDEN STADIUM

There's more to Ohio than the Buckeyes, so make sure you show the Bobcats some attention too. Ohio Bobcats football began in 1894 and since then their championship records are pretty long, getting to multiple bowl games along the way. Peden Stadium, where the Bobcats play, has been designated an official Ohio historical site.

Website: www.ohiobobcats.com/navbar-sports

Contact: Peden Stadium, 200 Richland Ave., Athens OH 45701; (740) 593-1000.

XAVIER UNIVERSITY MUSKETEERS / CINTAS CENTER

The Xavier Musketeers men's basketball team hasn't made the Final Four, but has 27 tournament wins in 27 appearances. They play their games at the Cintas Center.

Website: https://goxavier.com and www.cintascenter.com

Info: Tours of the Cintas Center can be arranged in advance by calling (513) 745-3394.

Contact: Cintas Center, 1624 Herald Ave., Cincinnati OH 45207; (513) 745-3428.

DAYTON RACING

Dayton Raceway is located at Hollywood Gaming, where you can play the slots or a few hands of poker after watching live harness racing. The season runs from September to December, so check the website for the most up-to-date schedule.

Website: https://www.hollywooddaytonraceway.com/racing

Contact: Dayton Racing, 777 Hollywood Blvd., Dayton OH 45414; (937) 235-7800.

JACK NICKLAUS MUSEUM

Jack Nicklaus once said: "Success depends almost entirely on how effectively you learn to manage the game's two ultimate adversaries: the course and yourself." He did both beautifully. The Golden Bear was one of the greatest golfers of all time, winning a record 18 major championships. The 12,000-square-foot museum, which is on the campus of Ohio State University, honors the man, his career, and his legend.

Website: https://www.nicklausmuseum.org

Info: The Museum is open Tuesday through Saturday 9 a.m. to 5 p.m. and is closed on Sunday and Monday. Cost: adults, $10; students, $5 (w/valid ID).

Contact: Jack Nicklaus Museum, 2355 Olentangy River Rd., Columbus OH 43210; (614) 247-5959.

Did you know? The Toledo Mud Hens, who were often cheered on by Max Klinger on *M*A*S*H*, are a real minor-league baseball team? You can see them play a game on your trip to Ohio. Buy a ticket and support them! For more information visit https://www.milb.com/toledo.

OKLAHOMA

What can you say about Oklahoma? Well, it's the home state of the legendary baseball player Mickey Mantle. It's also home to the University of Oklahoma Sooners and is considered the softball capital of the world.

NATIONAL SOFTBALL HALL OF FAME AND MUSEUM

I played softball as a kid and absolutely loved it, and the game holds a special place in my heart. Oklahoma is considered the softball capital of the world and is home to the ASA Hall of Fame Complex, where the NCAA Women's College World Series (WCWS), the World Cup of Softball, Border Battle, the USA Softball 18U GOLD National Championship, and the USA Softball Slow Pitch Championship Series take place. The National Softball Hall of Fame and Museum is a great venue to learn more about the sport and those who made it famous. Definitely worth a visit.

Website: https://www.teamusa.org/usa-softball/national-softball-hall-of-fame

Info: The Hall of Fame and Museum is open Monday through Friday 8:30 a.m. to 4:30 p.m. Check the USA Softball Hall of Fame Complex for weekend hours. Cost: free, but donations are welcome.

Contact: National Softball Hall of Fame and Museum, 2801 NE 50th St., Oklahoma City OK 73111; (405) 424-5266.

NATIONAL WRESTLING HALL OF FAME AND MUSEUM

There are two National Wrestling Hall of Fame locations—the other is in Waterloo, Iowa. There is information on wrestling throughout the ages as well as exhibits on amateur and Olympic wrestling.

Website: https://nwhof.org/stillwater

Contact: National Wrestling Hall of Fame and Museum, 405 W Hall of Fame Ave., Stillwater OK 74075; (405) 377-5243.

OKLAHOMA SPORTS HALL OF FAME / OKLAHOMA TENNIS HALL OF FAME

Oklahoma! Where the wind comes sweepin'—oh you probably know how it goes, but it's also Oklahoma where the sports are plentiful and the athletes need to be honored. They are honored here at the Oklahoma Sports Hall of Fame, where you'll find the Jim Thorpe Museum. Thorpe grew up in the Sac and Fox Nation in Oklahoma and became an Olympic gold medalist in the 1912 pentathlon and decathlon. He was a versatile athlete, playing football (collegiate and professional), professional baseball, and basketball.

Website: https://www.oklahomasportshalloffame.org

Contact: Oklahoma Sports Hall of Fame, 20 S Mickey Mantle Dr., Bricktown, Oklahoma City OK 73104; (405) 427-1400.

> **Good Eats**
> When you're hungry, take a break and eat at Mickey Mantle's Steakhouse, named by his family and steakhouse owners Jim Ingram and Monte Hough, who wanted to honor "The Commerce Comet." Visit https://mickeymantlesteakhouse.com for more information. The restaurant is at 7 S Mickey Mantle Dr., Oklahoma City OK 73104; (405) 272-0777.
>
> How about some barbecue instead? Billy Sims, who played at the University of Oklahoma, won the Heisman Trophy, and played for the Detroit Lions in the NFL, now owns Billy Sims BBQ. There are eight locations throughout Oklahoma, so visit www.billysimsbbq.com for more information.

OKLAHOMA CITY THUNDER / CHESAPEAKE ENERGY ARENA

This NBA franchise was once called the Seattle SuperSonics and won a championship back in 1979. This is where famed NBA players Kevin Durant and Russell Westbrook got their starts. NBA star Chris Paul and the rest of the Thunder play at the Chesapeake Energy Arena.

Website: https://www.nba.com/thunder and https://www.chesapeakearena.com

Contact: Chesapeake Energy Arena, 100 W Reno Ave., Oklahoma City OK 73102; (405) 602-8700.

COLLEGE SPORTS TOUR

OKLAHOMA SOONERS / GAYLORD FAMILY OKLAHOMA MEMORIAL STADIUM

Talk about records—606 wins, seven national championships, seven Heisman Trophy winners (to date)— and the Oklahoma Sooners football team, which began in 1895, just keeps going. The Sooners play their home games at Gaylord Family Oklahoma Memorial Stadium, which is considered among the 15 largest college football stadiums in the nation.

Website: www.soonersports.com

Contact: Gaylord Family Oklahoma Memorial Stadium, 1185 Asp Ave., Norman OK 73019; (405) 325-2424.

OKLAHOMA STATE UNIVERSITY COWBOYS / BOONE PICKENS STADIUM

So far the Cowboys have wrangled themselves 10 conference titles, and the orange and black are worth the ticket. If you want to know more about their history and accomplishments, check out their Heritage Hall, where you can see memorabilia and memories from 1890 to the present.

Website: https://okstate.com

Info: Heritage Hall is open from 8 a.m. to 5 p.m.

Contact: Boone Pickens Stadium, 700 W Hall of Fame Ave., Stillwater OK 74075; (877) 255-4678.

OREGON

Let's first get the pronunciation out of the way so when you're there, you don't sound like you don't belong. The correct pronunciation is "OR," "ih," and "gun." Now that we've gotten that out of the way, there are plenty of professional and college sports teams for you to root for. Don't just choose one—see them all!

Did you know? The Oregon Sports Hall of Fame and Museum has a few exhibits on display at their location. Call ahead of time (503-227-7466) to make sure the displays are still available. The museum is located at 4840 SW Western Ave., Beaverton OR 97005. The museum is open between 9 a.m. and 2 p.m. Monday through Friday. Visit http://oregonsportshall.org for more information. There is no charge for admission.

COLLEGE SPORTS TOUR

UNIVERSITY OF OREGON DUCKS / AUTZEN STADIUM

They were once known as the Webfoots back in the early 1900s, but today they are the Oregon Ducks with such graduates as Heisman Trophy winner Marcus Mariota and Pro Football Hall of Fame quarterback Dan Fouts. The Ducks play their football games at Autzen Stadium. Their archrivals are the Oregon State Beavers, and the two teams have been playing annually for more than 125 years. The Ducks currently lead the competition.

Website: https://goducks.com/sports

Contact: Autzen Stadium, 2700 Martin Luther King Jr. Blvd., Eugene OR 97401; (541) 346-4461.

Did you know? If Faber College Football Stadium in the 1978 film *National Lampoon's Animal House* looks familiar, that's because the filming took place at the University of Oregon's Autzen Stadium.

OREGON STATE UNIVERSITY BEAVERS / RESER STADIUM

The Oregon State Beavers have won five conference football titles, making them a requirement to watch when you're in town. They play at Reser Stadium.

Website: https://osubeavers.com

Contact: Reser Stadium, 660 SW 26th St., Corvallis OR 97331; (541) 737-2547.

PORTLAND TRAIL BLAZERS / MODA CENTER

The year this book comes out—2020—the Portland Trail Blazers will be celebrating their 50th anniversary. During this half-century, they have won the NBA championship once, back in 1977, and, to date, have qualified for the playoffs in 34 of 48 seasons.

They play at the Moda Center, which was once known as—and probably always will be—the Rose Garden. At press time, no tours were available, but it was said that the tours would start again later in 2019, so check the website for up-to-date information.

Website: https://www.nba.com/blazers

Contact: Moda Center, One Center Court, Suite 150, Portland OR 97227; (503) 235-8771.

PORTLAND TIMBERS / PROVIDENCE PARK

The Portland Timbers just celebrated their 10th anniversary in 2019 and became MLS champions in 2015. They play in Providence Park, which they share with Portland Thorns FC, a team in the National Women's Soccer League. Providence Park has so much history to it, you'll definitely want a ticket to get into the venue. Don't believe me? Here are just a few things that have happened here: President William H. Taft visited in 1909, "The King" Elvis Presley performed here, and the 2003 FIFA Women's World Cup, the 2009 Cricket Wireless Triple-A All-Star Game, and the final professional game for soccer legend Pelé in the North American Soccer League's Soccer Bowl '77 were held here.

Website: https://www.timbers.com

Contact: Providence Park, 1844 SW Morrison St., Portland OR 97205; (503) 553-5400.

WORLD OF SPEED

Fast cars—that's all that matters at the World of Speed. It's all about race cars, motorcycles, and boats. Here you can drive a race car simulator and see many exhibits that show you the history and accomplishments of those in their sports. You will just say "too sweet" when you check out these cars. There's also the Mario Andretti: Racing Royalty exhibit, which includes everything from his first race car to his 1967 Ford GT40 Mk IV Sebring winner. They also celebrate women in racing—as they should.

Website: www.worldofspeed.org

Info: The World of Speed is closed on Monday, and open Tuesday through Friday 10 a.m. to 5 p.m., Saturday 9 a.m. to 5 p.m., and Sunday 10 a.m. to 5 p.m. Cost: adults, $10; seniors, students, veterans, and active military (w/valid ID), $8.50; youth (ages 6–12), $5; children 5 and under, free.

Contact: World of Speed, 27490 SW 95th Ave., Wilsonville OR 97070; (503) 563-6444.

PENNSYLVANIA

Pennsylvania is filled with the rich history of the United States, including Independence Hall and the Liberty Bell. There are mountains, farms, and small and big cities, but when sports fans think of Pennsylvania, there is plenty to think about. From the college towns to the professional sports teams—and even the iconic movie scene in *Rocky* where he runs up the steps—Pennsylvania is a sports lover's travel dream.

PITTSBURGH STEELERS / HEINZ FIELD

You're in Steelers Nation now! It's the oldest franchise in the AFC, dating back to 1933. They have won six Super Bowls, the latest in 2008. Football greats such as "Mean" Joe Greene, Franco Harris, Ben Roethlisberger, and Terry Bradshaw have donned the black and gold. In the 1970s, their defensive line was known as the "Steel Curtain" and included Greene, L. C. Greenwood, Ernie Holmes, and Dwight White.

The Steelers play at Heinz Field and behind-the-scenes tours are available. You'll see the locker room, press box, field level, and much more. They also offer a special celebration tour if you're enjoying a special day.

Website: https://www.steelers.com and https://heinzfield.com

Info: Heinz Field tours are offered from April 1 through October 31. Costs were due to go up in 2019, so check the website for the most updated information.

Contact: Heinz Field Stadium, 100 Art Rooney Ave., Pittsburgh PA 15212; (412) 323-1200.

THE HISTORY CENTER

Want to learn more about the Pittsburgh Steelers and the history of Pennsylvania football? Take a trip to the Western Pennsylvania Sports Museum at the History Center. Here you'll learn about the history of the Steelers' six Super Bowl trophies and learn about Friday Night Lights. Get a close-up look at team uniforms and equipment, try on a Super Bowl ring, and throw the pigskin.

Website: https://www.heinzhistorycenter.org/exhibits/super-steelers

Info: The center is open 10 a.m. to 5 p.m. daily. Cost: adults, $18; seniors (ages 62 and older), $15; retired and active duty military receive $2 off of admission; students w/valid school ID, $9; children (ages 6–17), $9; children 5 and under, free.

Contact: Heinz History Center, 1212 Smallman St., Pittsburgh PA 15222; (412) 454-6000.

PHILADELPHIA EAGLES / LINCOLN FINANCIAL FIELD

The Philadelphia Eagles won Super Bowl LII in 2017, and it was their first Super Bowl victory. The Eagles play at Lincoln Financial Field, which offers behind-the-scenes tours. When it comes to rivalries, it's all about the New York Giants.

Website: https://www.philadelphiaeagles.com and https://www.lincolnfinancialfield.com

Info: Cost: adults, $15; children (ages 4 and older) and seniors, $10.

Contact: Lincoln Financial Field, 1 Lincoln Financial Field Way, Philadelphia PA 19148; (267) 570-4000.

PHILADELPHIA FLYERS / WELLS FARGO CENTER

The Philadelphia Flyers were part of the 1967 NHL expansion. They won the Stanley Cup in 1974 and 1975. On their behind-the-scenes tours of the Wells Fargo Center you'll see how the Flyers ice is installed and see the opponents' locker room and the press box area.

Website: https://www.nhl.com/flyers and https://www.wellsfargocenterphilly.com/teams/detail/philadelphia-flyers

Info: Wells Fargo Center tours are approximately 60 to 90 minutes long. The stadium tour dates are announced each season, so check the website for more information.

Contact: Wells Fargo Center, 3601 S Broad St., Philadelphia PA 19148; (215) 336-3600.

PITTSBURGH PENGUINS / PPG PAINTS ARENA

After being founded in 1967, the NHL's Pittsburgh Penguins are now owned by the former legendary Penguin "Super" Mario Lemieux. In 1993, the Penguins won the franchise's first-ever Presidents' Trophy for being the team with the most points at the end of the regular season. They've won the Stanley Cup five times, the latest as back-to-back championships in 2016 and 2017. They play at PPG Paints Arena, which offers behind-the-scenes tours.

Website: https://www.nhl.com/penguins and www.ppgpaintsarena.com

Info: PPG Paints Arena tours include the Captain Morgan and Lexus Clubs, a Jim Beam Make History Suite, select locker rooms, and more.

Contact: PPG Paints Arena, 1001 Fifth Ave., Pittsburgh PA 15219; (412) 642-1800.

PHILADELPHIA PHILLIES / CITIZENS BANK PARK

When I first started loving baseball, I was always a Mets fan, but I always got a kick out of the Philadelphia Phillies mascot, the Phillie Phanatic (just don't tell the Mets fan that). What a goofball—he always made the game a ton of fun. The Philadelphia Phillies have won two World Series championships, the latest by defeating the Tampa Bay Rays in 2008, and seven National League pennants. They play at Citizens Bank Park, which offers behind-the-scenes tours.

Website: https://www.mlb.com/phillies

Info: Tours are offered in season (April to September). Public tours are offered Monday through Saturday. Non–game day tours are at 10:30 a.m. Game day tours are at 10:30 a.m. and 12:30 p.m. Tours are not available on days when the Phillies have a home afternoon game. Offseason (October–March) public tours are offered at 10:30 a.m. Monday, Wednesday, and Friday.

Contact: Citizens Bank Park, 1 Citizens Bank Way, Philadelphia PA 19148; (215) 463-1000.

PITTSBURGH PIRATES / PNC PARK

Way back in 1881, the Pittsburgh Pirates were founded. You can call them the "Bucs" or the "Buccos," but you can also call them World Series champions. They have won five of them in their history, including the famous 1979 World Series where the "We Are Family" theme song from Sister Sledge carried them all the way. But those striped baseball caps! The Pirates play at PNC Park, which offers behind-the-scenes tours.

Website: https://www.mlb.com/pirates

Info: The Pirates behind-the-scenes tours of PNC Park can be done before the game as well. The tours last 60 to 100 minutes, depending on the timing of batting practice. Cost: adults, $10; seniors (ages 55 and older) and children/students (ages 6–14), $8; children 5 and under, free.

Contact: PNC Park, 115 Federal St., Pittsburgh PA 15212; (412) 321-BUCS.

PHILADELPHIA 76ERS / WELLS FARGO CENTER

The NBA's Philadelphia 76ers were founded in 1945 and have included such legendary players as Wilt Chamberlain, Hal Greer, Billy Cunningham, Julius Erving, Andrew Toney, Moses Malone, Charles Barkley, and Allen Iverson. They have won three NBA championships in their history. In 2019, Barkley took his place as the eighth Sixer to be immortalized with a statue on Legends Walk, so check that out before the game.

Website: https://www.nba.com/sixers and https://www.wellsfargocenterphilly.com/teams/detail/philadelphia-76ers

Info: Wells Fargo Center Tours are approximately 60 to 90 minutes long. The stadium tour dates are announced each season, so check the website for more information.

Contact: Wells Fargo Center, 3601 S Broad St., Philadelphia PA 19148; (215) 336-3600.

THE CLEMENTE MUSEUM

Roberto Clemente was drafted in 1954 at a time when racial prejudice was running rampant. He fought through it and also became one of the greatest ballplayers of all time. This museum honors the contributions of this great man, and includes photographs and artifacts. There is art, literature, and other memorabilia about his life and his community work.

Website: https://www.clementemuseum.com/museum

Info: The Clemente Museum is open by appointment only for guided tours. All tours require a reservation.

Contact: The Clemente Museum, 3339 Penn Ave., Pittsburgh PA 15201; (412) 621-1268.

WORLD OF LITTLE LEAGUE MUSEUM

Raise your hand if you played in Little League when you were a kid. (Me!) Raise your hand if you think that practically every MLB player did the same years before they hit the big leagues. (Me!). This museum honors the history of Little League baseball and softball. Everyone started somewhere, right? There are hundreds of baseball artifacts to look at during your tour, where you can learn about the story of Little League, see interactive exhibits, and add your own photos into the museum!

Website: https://www.littleleague.org/world-of-little-league

Info: The museum is open every day from 9 a.m. until 5 p.m., with extended hours during the Little League Baseball World Series. Cost: general admission, $5; seniors (ages 62 and over), $3; children (ages 5–12), $2; children 5 and under, free;

Info: World of Little League Museum, 525 US-15, South Williamsport PA 17702; (570) 326-3607.

COLLEGE SPORTS TOUR

PENNSYLVANIA STATE UNIVERSITY NITTANY LIONS / BEAVER STADIUM

My friends love the Nittany Lions, my family loves the Nittany Lions, and I have a small Nittany Lion stuffed animal in my daughter's room. Whether you're watching the basketball team while sitting in the Legion of Blue or cheering on their football team, you'll feel like part of the family. The football team plays at Beaver Stadium, which offers behind-the-scenes tours of the media room, home locker room, tunnel and field, and recruiting and club areas. The basketball team plays at the Bryce Jordan Center.

Website: https://gopsusports.com

Info: Cost: Tickets for the Beaver Stadium tours are $20 for adults and $15 for students, seniors, and Friends of the Penn State All-Sports Museum. Children 3 and under are free. Some walk-up tickets may be available for $25 per person. Tickets to the general public will be available about three weeks prior to each tour.

Contact: Beaver Stadium, 1 Beaver Stadium, University Park PA 16802; (814) 863-1000.

UNIVERSITY OF PITTSBURGH PANTHERS / HEINZ FIELD

The Pittsburgh Panthers football team has claimed nine national championships. Pitt plays home games at Heinz Field, which they share with the National Football League Pittsburgh Steelers, and utilizes the University of Pittsburgh Medical Center Sports Performance Complex as their practice facility.

Website: https://heinzfield.com

Info: Heinz Field tours are offered from April 1 through October 31. Costs were due to go up in 2019, so check the website for the most updated information.

Contact: Heinz Field Stadium, 100 Art Rooney Ave., Pittsburgh PA 15212; (412) 323-1200.

TEMPLE UNIVERSITY OWLS / LINCOLN FINANCIAL FIELD

Whooo are the Temple University Owls? They are archrivals of the Villanova Wildcats, whom they face each year in the Mayor's Cup game for Philadelphia-area bragging rights. They won their last division title in 2015. They play their games at Lincoln Financial Field, home to the Philadelphia Eagles, which offers behind-the-scenes tours of the stadium. They won their last conference title in 2016.

Website: https://owlsports.com and https://www.lincolnfinancialfield.com

Info: Cost: adults, $15; children and seniors, $10.

Contact: Lincoln Financial Field, 1 Lincoln Financial Field Way, Philadelphia PA 19148; (267) 570-4000.

Statue Alert!

Put your arms over your head, take a deep breath, and start running up the 72 stone steps that are located outside the entrance of the Philadelphia Museum of Art. Art and sports? Yup. Now if you play the song "Gonna Fly Now," you just might see where I'm going with this. The Philadelphia Museum of Art is home to the steps that Rocky Balboa ran up in the movie *Rocky* and where you'll find the statue dedicated to this fictional boxer.

WEBSITE: www.philamuseum.org

CONTACT: 2600 Benjamin Franklin Pkwy., Philadelphia PA 19130; (215) 763-8100.

VILLANOVA UNIVERSITY WILDCATS / VILLANOVA STADIUM

Speaking of the Wildcats, their Mayor's Cup game with Temple is not their only annual grudge match. They also play in the Battle of the Blue against the University of Delaware Fightin' Blue Hens. Maybe you can catch this matchup on your college sports tour.

If you prefer hoops, the Wildcats men's basketball team is worth your attention, especially after winning the National Championship in 2018. They play some of their games at Wells Fargo Center and some of them at the Finneran Pavilion, so make sure you know which venue you need to go to. Wells Fargo does offer behind-the-scenes tours, so check that out while you're there.

Website: https://www.wellsfargocenterphilly.com

Info: Wells Fargo Center tours are approximately 60 to 90 minutes long. The stadium tour dates are announced each season, so check the website for more information.

Contact: Wells Fargo Center, 3601 S Broad St., Philadelphia PA 19148; (215) 336-3600.

Did you know? Foxburg Country Club (369 Harvey Road, Foxburg PA 16036; 724-659-3196; www.foxburgcountryclub.com) is the oldest golf course in the United States that is in continuous use. It's open to the public.

RHODE ISLAND

Rhode Island is the smallest state in the United States, and is home to beautiful Gilded Age mansions as well as the popular Block Island. And it's home to two colleges that should be on your sports tour.

COLLEGE SPORTS TOUR

UNIVERSITY OF RHODE ISLAND RAMS / MEADE STADIUM

The Rams first hit the field back in 1895. Today they play their games at Meade Stadium in Kingston. The Rams basketball team was the 2018 conference champion. Depending on the season, check out either a Rams basketball or football game.

Website: www.gorhody.com

Contact: 5 W Alumni Ave., Kingston RI 02881; (401) 874-5210.

PROVIDENCE COLLEGE FRIARS / DUNKIN' DONUTS CENTER

The Friars basketball team is rebuilding and definitely deserves a visit. They play at the Dunkin' Donuts Center in Providence.

Website: https://friars.com and www.dunkindonutscenter.com

Contact: Dunkin' Donuts Center, 1 LaSalle Square, Providence RI 02903; (401) 331-6700.

You'll score an ace if you visit the International Tennis Hall of Fame in Newport. Well not really, but you'll have a ton of fun. WIKIMEDIA COMMONS

INTERNATIONAL TENNIS HALL OF FAME

Did you ever get a chance to watch Arthur Ashe play tennis? Maybe you're a huge Serena or Venus Williams fan? Perhaps you just want to learn about the history of this sport, which includes such legends as Billie Jean King and Bjorn Borg. It's an incredible museum, and if you want to enhance your experience, time your visit to the Enshrinement Weekend (typically in July), when some of the greats of the sport are honored.

Website: https://www.tennisfame.com

Info: Cost: adults, $15; seniors (ages 62 and over), students, military, and USTA and AAA members, $12; children 16 and under, free. Although the museum is self-guided, there are tours available at 11 a.m. and 2 p.m. daily, from July to September, and on weekends only in June and October.

Contact: International Tennis Hall of Fame, 194 Bellevue Ave., Newport RI 02840; (401) 849-3990.

SOUTH CAROLINA

With its miles of coastline, gardens, historic sites, and plantations, South Carolina is a gorgeous place to visit. For sports fans, it's even more fun to sit back and watch the races—horse races or car races, whatever gets your fancy.

AIKEN THOROUGHBRED RACING HALL OF FAME AND MUSEUM

Horses are beautiful animals and watching them race is watching poetry in motion. This hall of fame and museum celebrates this sport and the thoroughbreds that have made it famous, including flat racers and steeplechase horses, from 1942 through the present. You can see photos, trophies, and other memorabilia. Enjoy the Courtyard of Champions and the trophy collection as well as Dogwood Stable.

> **Website:** https://www.aikenracinghalloffame.com
>
> **Info:** The Museum is open Tuesday through Friday 2 p.m. to 5 p.m., Saturday 10 a.m. to 5 p.m., and Sunday 2 p.m. to 5 pm. Cost: Admission is free, but donations are always welcome.
>
> **Contact:** Aiken Thoroughbred Racing Hall of Fame and Museum, 135 Dupree Place SW (inside historic Hopelands Gardens), Aiken SC 29801; (803) 642-7631.

DARLINGTON RACEWAY / STOCK CAR MUSEUM

Maybe you prefer to watch stock cars race and not horses? Or maybe you watch both? Either way, the Darlington Raceway and their Stock Car Museum is an ideal stop. Whether you're there for a race—such as their NASCAR races—or are just there for the museum, you'll have a blast. You'll see old and new cars and learn about the man behind the museum—Joe Weatherly, who the museum was originally named after. Weatherly was known as "The Clown Prince of Stock Car Racing," but was tragically killed during a race. The museum is about the history of Darlington Raceway and the sport in general.

You can also see a section dedicated to the National Motorsports Press Association (NMPA) Hall of Fame, filled with photos, memorabilia, and interactive exhibits.

> **Website:** www.darlingtonraceway.com
>
> **Info:** The Darlington Raceway Stock Car Museum, NMPA Hall of Fame, and Darlington Raceway gift shop are open 10 a.m. to 4 p.m. Monday through Friday. Cost: adults, $7.50; military, $5; children 12 and under, free.
>
> **Contact:** Darlington Raceway, 1301 Harry Byrd Hwy., Darlington SC 29532; (843) 395-8900.

SHOELESS JOE JACKSON MUSEUM AND LIBRARY

South Carolina doesn't have any professional baseball teams, but that's okay because what it does have is a museum dedicated to "Shoeless" Joe Jackson, who was born and died in South Carolina. The outfielder was allegedly part of the Black Sox Scandal, a conspiracy to fix the World Series by the 1919 Chicago White Sox. The Museum is located in the house where Joe lived and died.

Website: www.shoelessjoejackson.org

Info: The Shoeless Joe Jackson Museum and Library is open on Saturday from 10 a.m. to 2 p.m.

Contact: Shoeless Joe Jackson Museum and Library, 356 Field St., across from Fluor Field, Historic West End, Greenville SC 29601; (864) 346-4867.

Did you know? The movie *Field of Dreams*, which was based on the book *Shoeless Joe* by W. P. Kinsella, is about an Iowa farmer who hears a mysterious voice that instructs him to build a baseball field on his farm so Shoeless Joe can play baseball again.

COLLEGE SPORTS TOUR

UNIVERSITY OF SOUTH CAROLINA GAMECOCKS

They are named after Revolutionary War hero Thomas Sumter, who was called the "Carolina Gamecock" for his fighting style. The stadium they play in, Williams-Brice Stadium, is one of just two stadiums in FBS named for a woman. Martha Williams-Brice left the majority of her estate to the university.

Website: https://gamecocksonline.com

Contact: Williams-Brice Stadium, 1125 George Rogers Blvd., Columbia SC 29201; (803) 777-4271.

CLEMSON UNIVERSITY FIGHTING TIGERS / MEMORIAL STADIUM

Over 700 wins? You read that right. The Clemson Tigers football team is one of the most popular football teams in the country, so make sure you check out a game and see what all the worthy fuss is about. Is it all because of a rock? Yup, you read that right too. It's not really, but there is a famous Howard's Rock named for Frank Howard, who received it from a friend of his who said "Here's a rock from Death Valley, California, to Death Valley, South Carolina." The rock meant nothing for a while until Howard wanted to get rid of it. It was put on a pedestal, and the players happened to touch it before they beat their rival team. That began the tradition of rubbing the rock, which dates back to 1967. That's only part of the Clemson fun— oh yeah, there's football too!

Want to watch the Tigers play hoops? Check out the Clemson Tigers basketball team and you won't be disappointed.

Website: https://clemsontigers.com

Contact: Memorial Stadium, 1 Avenue of Champions, Clemson SC 29634; (800) 253-6766; Littlejohn Coliseum (basketball), 219 Perimeter Rd., Clemson SC 29634.

SOUTH DAKOTA

Known for its mountains, desert, rolling plains, small towns, and historic buildings, South Dakota is mostly known for the four US presidents carved into stone at Mount Rushmore and the Crazy Horse Memorial, a tribute to the state's Native American roots. When it comes to sports, it's all about college sports and the rodeo.

CASEY TIBBS SOUTH DAKOTA RODEO CENTER

Truth be told, I don't know a ton about the rodeo, except that I love watching it. This museum honors the rodeo and especially Casey Tibbs, who in 1949, at the tender age of 19, became the youngest man ever to win the national saddle bronc-riding crown. The museum has memorabilia of nine-time world champion Tibbs as well as 1920s trick rider Mattie Goff Newcombe. You can ride a virtual reality bronc and see a display of saddles.

Statue Alert!

There are also five large bronze statues of rodeo champs at the Casey Tibbs South Dakota Rodeo Center.

Website: www.caseytibbs.com

Info: September through May the museum is open Tuesday through Friday 10 a.m. to 5 p.m., Saturday 10 a.m. to 3 p.m, closed Sunday and Monday. June through August it is open Monday through Friday 9 a.m. to 5 p.m., Saturday 10 a.m. to 5 p.m., and Sunday 1 p.m. to 5 p.m. Cost: adults, $6; seniors (ages 55 and older), $5; veterans and children (ages 6–18), $4; children 5 and under, free.

Contact: Casey Tibbs South Dakota Rodeo Center, 210 Verendrye Dr., Ft. Pierre SD 57532; (605) 494-1094.

COLLEGE SPORTS TOUR

SOUTH DAKOTA STATE JACKRABBITS

Website: https://gojacks.com

TENNESSEE

The beautiful Tennessee mountains, vast farmland, and the rich history of country and jazz music make this state feel like a big ol' bowl of southern comfort. Visitors love the races, football games, and college sports teams too. It's a great combination that makes Tennessee a must-see state. I volunteer to go again! (It's nicknamed the Volunteer State.)

TENNESSEE TITANS / NISSAN STADIUM

Remember the Houston Oilers (in Texas)? Well now they are the Tennessee Titans. Sometimes it's hard to keep straight when teams move to different cities and states, but just remember that they went to the Super Bowl the same year they changed their name to the Titans. Unfortunately, they didn't get the "W," but you should still root them on and take a tour of the Nissan Stadium that they play in. They are a fierce team, so if you're in Titan country, stop by and see a game. On a 60-minute behind-the-scenes tour, you'll see the Titans locker room, press box, the playing field, TRac's Den, the cheerleader locker room, and more.

Website: https://www.titansonline.com

Info: Nissan Stadium tours are held on Wednesday and Friday at 2 p.m. and on certain Saturdays at noon. Cost: adults, $12; students, seniors, and military, $10.

Contact: Nissan Stadium, 1 Titans Way, Nashville TN 37213; (615) 565-4300.

NASHVILLE PREDATORS / BRIDGESTONE ARENA

It was 1998 when the Nashville Predators came onto the NHL scene. In 2017, they made it to their first Stanley Cup Finals. Fans love their team and have started a tradition of throwing an octopus or a catfish (not real, of course) onto the ice to show support. They play at the Bridgestone Arena.

Website: https://www.nhl.com/predators and https://www.bridgestonearena.com

Contact: Bridgestone Arena, 501 Broadway, Nashville TN 37203; (615) 770-2000.

COLLEGE SPORTS TOUR

University of Tennessee Volunteers / Neyland Stadium

Tennessee has won six national championships! If you're visiting, consider partici-pating in the Vol Walk, which started back in 1988, when thousands of fans line the street to shake the players' hands as they walk into Neyland Stadium. I'm telling you, the energy at a college football game is like no other. The stadium offers behind-the-scenes tours by appointment only and they must be scheduled five business days in advance, so plan ahead. They include General Neyland's statue (selfie alert!), the Peyton Manning Locker Complex, Wolf Kaplan Center, and more.

Website: https://utsports.com

Info: Sixty-minute stadium tours are available Monday through Thursday by appointment only. Cost: Groups of up to 20, $8 per person. Groups of more than 20, $150 flat rate.

Contact: Neyland Stadium, 1300 Phillip Fulmer Way, Knoxville TN 37916; (865) 974-1224.

University of Memphis Tigers / Liberty Bowl Stadium

When you watch the Tigers play, you might want to show up a few hours before the game and line up outside the stadium for the "Tiger Walk." The adrenaline is contagious! The Memphis Tigers play at the Liberty Bowl Memorial Stadium, but it doesn't offer any behind-the-scenes tours right now.

Website: https://gotigersgo.com and www.thelibertybowlstadium.com

Contact: Liberty Bowl Stadium, 335 South Hollywood St., Memphis TN 38104; (901) 729-4344.

MEMPHIS GRIZZLIES / FEDEXFORUM

The NBA's Memphis Grizzlies originally came into the league as the Vancouver Griz-zlies and moved to Memphis almost 20 years ago. They play their games at the FedExForum, which offers behind-the-scenes tours.

Website: https://www.nba.com/grizzlies and https://fedexforum.com

Info: FedExForum tours are only available for groups of 10 or more, Monday through Friday between 9 a.m. and 4 p.m. only on days when events are not scheduled. All groups *must* schedule a tour in advance. Individuals can be added on to tours, but you must call to find out the schedule. Cost: adults, $5; seniors, $4; students (ages 12 and under), $3.

Contact: FedExForum, 191 Beale St., Memphis TN 38103; (901) 205-2525.

MEMPHIS INTERNATIONAL RACEWAY

And they're off! At Memphis International Raceway, there are many races for you to watch—too many to mention here, that's for sure—so be sure to check out the schedule before you plan your vacation. Good news! At the Memphis International Raceway, all tickets to MIR's Dragstrip are a PIT Pass, so you will have the ability to get up close with all drivers/cars.

Website: www.racemir.com

Contact: Memphis International Raceway, 5500 Victory Ln., Millington TN 38053; (901) WOW-RACE.

WOMEN'S BASKETBALL HALL OF FAME

It has the world's largest basketball, a place to dribble and pass, and the 17-foot Eastman Statue. The Women's Basketball Hall of Fame also tells the story of the women who have had an impact on this sport. It's a must-see for any sports fan.

Website: https://www.wbhof.com

Info: From Labor Day to April 30 the Hall of Fame is open Tuesday through Friday 11 a.m. to 5 p.m. and Saturday 10 a.m. to 5 p.m. From May 1 to Labor Day, hours are Monday through Saturday 10 a.m. to 5 p.m. Cost: adults, $7.95; seniors (ages 62 and older), $5.95; youth (6–15), $5.95; children under 5, free.

Contact: Women's Basketball Hall of Fame, 700 Hall of Fame Dr., Knoxville TN 37915; (865) 633-9000.

Nancy Dunkle, Nancy Lieberman, and Rebecca Lobo are just a few of the athletes recognized at the National Women's Basketball Hall of Fame in Knoxville, a full interactive venue for all ages. WIKIMEDIA COMMONS

> ### Statue Alerts!
>
> I could go on and on about Pat Head Summitt to honor this legendary coach, but luckily there is a statue of her at Liberty Park to do the job. Here you'll also find a statue of Olympic gold medal winner Wilma Rudolph, considered the fastest woman in the world. In case, you didn't know, June 23 is Wilma Rudolph Day in her hometown of Clarksville.

TENNESSEE SPORTS HALL OF FAME

The Tennessee Sports Hall of Fame honors the state's sports history. You can see exhibits on Pat Summitt, Peyton Manning, and dress up like a Nashville Predator or a Tennessee Titan.

> **Website:** http://tshf.net
>
> **Info:** The Tennessee Sports Hall of Fame is open to the public Tuesday through Sunday 10 a.m. to 4 p.m. Cost: adults, $3; children, $2.
>
> **Contact:** Tennessee Sports Hall of Fame, Bridgestone Arena, 501 Broadway, Nashville TN 37203; (615) 242-4750.

>
>
> ### Good Eats
>
> Jerry "The King" Lawler made his mark on professional wrestling, and now he is making his mark on the culinary world with Jerry Lawler's Memphis BBQ. While you're traveling, take a break and chow down on a smoked salad, his signature BBQ, "Slamwiches," and "Tag Team Meals." There's even something for "little wrasslers."
>
> **WEBSITE:** www.jerrylawlerbbq.com
>
> **CONTACT:** King Jerry Lawler's Memphis BBQ Company, 465 North Germantown Pkwy. #116, Cordova TN 38018; (901) 509-2360.

TEXAS

Go big or go home! And when it comes to Texas sports, going big is where it's at!

PROFESSIONAL WRESTLING HALL OF FAME AND MUSEUM

As I've said before, I'm a huge professional wrestling fan and just seeing some of the memorabilia at this hall of fame and museum is a fun treat. Costumes, memories, and a wall of fame are a great way to preserve the history of professional wrestling. There are donations from such greats as David Von Erich (and all the Von Erichs) and so much more.

Website: https://www.pwhf.org

Info: The Hall of Fame and Museum is closed Monday, Tuesday, and Wednesday. It is open Thursday and Friday 10 a.m. to 3 p.m., Saturday 10 a.m. to 5 p.m., and Sunday 1 p.m. to 5 p.m. Let them know if you're coming on one of their closed days and they just might open the museum for you. Cost: regular admission, $3; seniors, $2; military (active/retired) and children 5 and under free.

Contact: Professional Wrestling Hall of Fame and Museum, 712 8th St., Suite 100, Wichita Falls TX 76301; (940) 264-8123.

INTERNATIONAL BOWLING MUSEUM AND HALL OF FAME

In case you didn't know, I authored a book on bowling. I've bowled in leagues for years, and my children started bowling probably before they even went to preschool. I also love watching it on television. We bowl for fun, and that's exactly why you should check out the International Bowling Museum and Hall of Fame. You'll learn the history of the sport and learn about those champions who have done so much for the sport. Strike!

Website: https://www.bowlingmuseum.com

Info: The Museum is open Tuesday through Saturday 9:30 a.m. to 5 p.m. and Sunday noon to 6 p.m. Closed Monday. Cost: adults, $9.50; seniors, $7.50; children (ages 4–18), $7.50; children 3 and under, free.

Contact: International Bowling Museum and Hall of Fame, 621 Six Flags Dr., Arlington TX 76011; (817) 385-8215.

BEN HOGAN MUSEUM OF DUBLIN

Born in Dublin, Texas, professional golfing legend Ben Hogan is honored in this small, but impressive museum.

> **Website:** https://benhoganmuseum.wixsite.com/benhoganmuseum
>
> **Info:** No admission charge.
>
> **Contact:** Ben Hogan Museum of Dublin, 121 E Blackjack St., Dublin TX 76446; (254) 445-4466.

TEXAS SPORTS HALL OF FAME

Wow. Remember the "Go big or go home" introduction to this chapter? Well here is a 35,000-square foot museum that is a big tribute to everyone at home in Texas. Who? How about Troy Aikman, Tom Landry, Roger Staubach, and Nolan Ryan, just to name a few.

> **Website:** www.tshof.org
>
> **Info:** The Hall of Fame is open Monday through Saturday 9 a.m. to 5 p.m. Cost: adults, $7; seniors (ages 60 and older), $6; students (1st through 12th grade), $3; children under 6, free.
>
> **Contact:** Texas Sports Hall of Fame, 1108 S University Parks Dr., Waco TX 76706; (254) 756-1633.

TEXAS TENNIS MUSEUM SPORTS HALL OF FAME

Tennis has an extensive history in Texas, and you can see it all for yourself at this museum.

> **Website:** https://www.texastennismuseum.org
>
> **Info:** The museum is open Monday through Saturday 9 a.m. to 5 p.m. Cost: adults, $7; seniors (ages 60 and older), $6; students (1st through 12th grade), $3; children under 6, USTA members, and active military, free.
>
> **Contact:** Texas Tennis Museum Sports Hall of Fame, 1108 S University Parks Dr., Waco TX 76706; (254) 756-1633.

NATIONAL SOCCER HALL OF FAME

If you call it soccer or call it football (or even *futbol*), and you absolutely love soccer, this hall of fame is for all fans of the beautiful sport. Here you can build your own national team, design your own MLS kit, play soccer through virtual reality, test your trivia knowledge, and more. The National Soccer Hall of Fame is in Frisco, on the south end of FC Stadium, the home of FC Dallas.

Website: https://www.nationalsoccerhof.com

Info: Monday and Tuesday, the Hall of Fame is closed. It is open Wednesday 1:30 p.m. to 9 p.m., Thursday 1:30 p.m. to 5:30 p.m., Friday 1:30 p.m. to 5:30 p.m., Saturday 10 a.m. to 5 p.m., and Sunday noon to 5 p.m. Cost: adults, $15; youth (ages 12 and under) and seniors, $12.

Contact: National Soccer Hall of Fame, 9200 World Cup Way, Ste. 600, Frisco TX 75033; (469) 365-0043.

FC DALLAS / TOYOTA STADIUM

Gooooooooaaaaalllllll! Practice yelling so you're ready when you see a soccer game and someone puts it in the net. FC Dallas was founded in 1995 as the Dallas Burn—what a name—before becoming FC Dallas. They play at Toyota Stadium.

Website: www.fcdallas.com

Contact: Toyota Stadium, 9200 World Cup Way, Frisco TX 75033; (214) 705-6700.

DALLAS COWBOYS / AT&T STADIUM

A shout-out to my mom, who has been the biggest Dallas Cowboys fan in my life. From the time I was little, she has been screaming and rooting for the Cowboys, starting with Roger Staubach. Even though I'm a Packers fan, I'll always have a place in my heart for the Cowboys just because of Mom.

That being said, the Dallas Cowboys have won five Super Bowls and it would be remiss of any football fan to not see a Cowboys game, if only because of the stadium and the history behind this NFL team. The Cowboys play at AT&T Stadium, where you can take a behind-the-scenes tour and see the Dallas Art Collection. You can take a VIP tour or a self-guided tour. On the self-guided tour, you get access to the field where you can run across it and throw a football or two, the Dallas Cowboys and the Cheerleaders locker rooms, and the postgame interview room. There are also Rally Day tours (game day tours).

Website: https://www.dallascowboys.com and https://attstadium.com/tours

Info: Tours are available Monday through Saturday 10 a.m. to 5 p.m. and Sunday 11 a.m. to 4 p.m. Cost: adults, $22; children/seniors, $17. Art tours: adults/children/seniors, $26.

Contact: AT&T Stadium, One AT&T Way, Arlington TX 76011; (817) 892-4000.

HOUSTON TEXANS / NRG PARK

The Texans are the youngest of Texas's football franchises, coming into the NFL in 2002 as an expansion team. They replaced the Houston Oilers, who are now the Tennessee Titans—keeping track of all of this? They haven't made it to the Super Bowl yet, but hey, they have plenty of time. In the meantime, the Houston Texans play at NRG Park. You can take a tour of this incredible stadium and see the field view, the visiting team's locker room, the press box, and so much more.

Website: https://www.houstontexans.com and https://www.nrgpark.com

Info: Stadium tours are available on Tuesday and Thursday at 10:15 a.m., noon, and 2 p.m., but check the website for availability. Cost: adults, $6; seniors and children (ages 3–12), $5; children 2 and under, free.

Contact: NRG Park, NRG Pkwy., Houston TX 77054; (832) 667-1400.

HOUSTON ASTROS / MINUTE MAID PARK

In 2017, the MLB's Houston Astros won their first World Series. It was a long time coming for a team that came into the league in 1962. It was the first World Series championship for the state of Texas too. If you want to see them play, you'll be heading to Minute Maid Park where you can take a behind-the-scenes tour. There are a variety of tours, including Classic, All-Star, and Ultimate Fan.

Website: https://www.mlb.com/astros

Info: The tour prices and schedule vary depending on the type of tour that you take, so check out the website for more information.

Contact: Minute Maid Park, 501 Crawford St., Houston TX 77002; (713) 259-8000.

TEXAS RANGERS / GLOBE LIFE PARK IN ARLINGTON

Fun fact—the Texas Rangers' first manager was Hall of Famer Ted Williams. Another fun fact—President George W. Bush headed the group that purchased the team in 1989 (he left once he was voted in as governor of Texas). Nolan Ryan is one of the legendary players who have worn the Rangers uniform. The Rangers play at Globe Life Park in Arlington, which offers public tours where you can see the batting cages, press box, luxury suites, dugouts, and more.

Website: https://www.mlb.com/rangers

Info: Tours are offered on non-game days Sunday 11 a.m. to 4 p.m. and Monday through Saturday 10 a.m. to 4 p.m. On game days tours are Monday through Saturday 10 a.m. to 2 p.m. (no tours Sunday). Cost: adults, $15; seniors, military, and first responders, $12; youth (ages 4–14), $10; children 3 and under, free.

Contact: Globe Life Park, 1000 Ballpark Way, Arlington TX 76011; (817) 273-5222.

DALLAS MAVERICKS / AMERICAN AIRLINES CENTER

Owned by the Shark Tank man himself, Mark Cuban, the NBA's Dallas Mavericks—you can call them the Mavs—have won one NBA championship (2011). The team plays its home games at the American Airlines Center, which it shares with the NHL's Dallas Stars. The American Airlines Center offers behind-the-scenes tours where you can see the press box, a luxury suite, party rooms, and more.

Website: https://www.mavs.com and www.americanairlinescenter.com

Info: Tours are scheduled by appointment only, Monday through Friday on non-event days. Tours are conducted at 10:30 a.m. and noon and are based on availability. Email tours@americanairlinescenter.com or call (214) 665-4210 to book your appointment. Reservations are accepted up to two months in advance with a minimum of one week notice. Cost: adults, $5; seniors, $4; children (ages 3–17), $3.

Contact: American Airlines Center, 2500 Victory Ave., Dallas TX 75219; (214) 222-3687.

SAN ANTONIO SPURS / AT&T CENTER

The San Antonio Spurs have five NBA championships to their name and they have me as a fan, so that says something, right? They play at the AT&T Center in San Antonio.

Website: https://www.nba.com/spurs and www.attcenter.com

Info: If you are interested in a tour of the AT&T Center, contact the Service Innovation Department at (210) 444-5140 or by email at serviceinnovation@attcenter.com.

Contact: 1 AT&T Center Pkwy., San Antonio TX 78219; (210) 444-5000.

DALLAS STARS / AMERICAN AIRLINES CENTER

The Dallas Stars came into the NHL in 1967 as the Minnesota North Stars. They won the Stanley Cup more than 30 years later, in 1999. The team plays its home games at the American Airlines Center, which it shares with the NBA's Dallas Mavericks. The American Airlines Center offers behind-the-scenes tours of the arena where you can see the press box, a luxury suite, party rooms, and more.

Website: www.americanairlinescenter.com

Info: Tours are scheduled by appointment only, Monday through Friday on non-event days. Tours are conducted at 10:30 a.m. and noon and are based on availability. Email tours@americanairlinescenter.com or call (214) 665-4210 to book your appointment. Reservations are accepted up to two months in advance with a minimum of one week notice. Cost: adults, $5; seniors, $4; children (ages 3–17), $3.

Contact: American Airlines Center, 2500 Victory Ave., Dallas TX 75219; (214) 222-3687.

HOUSTON DYNAMO / BBVA COMPASS STADIUM

Wow, how many teams can say they won the championship in both the first and second years of their history? Talk about making an impact! The Dynamo won the 2006 and 2007 MLS Cups and won the US Open Cup in 2018. They play at BBVA Compass Stadium.

> **Website:** https://www.houstondynamo.com and www.bbvacompassstadium.com
>
> Info: The Houston Dynamo only conduct group tours for parties of 10 or more. Tours are available Monday through Friday; no tours on game or event days.
>
> **Contact:** Houston Dynamo, 2200 Texas Ave., Houston TX 77003; (713) 547-3112.

COLLEGE SPORTS TOUR

BAYLOR UNIVERSITY BEARS / MCLANE STADIUM

The Baylor University Bears play at McLane Stadium, which offers 90-minute behind-the-scenes tours, and include the Baylor locker room, Presidential Level, press box, recruit lounge, suites, and field access. Cost: $10.20 per person.

> **Website:** https://baylorbears.com and www.mclanestadium.com
>
> **Contact:** McLane Stadium, 1001 South Martin Luther King Blvd., Waco TX 76704; (254) 710-1000.

UNIVERSITY OF HOUSTON COUGARS / TDECU STADIUM

> **Website:** https://uhcougars.com
>
> **Contact:** TDECU Stadium, 3875 Holman St., Houston TX 77004; (713) 743-9444.

UNIVERSITY OF TEXAS LONGHORNS / DARRELL K ROYAL–TEXAS MEMORIAL STADIUM

> **Website:** https://texassports.com
>
> **Contact:** 2139 San Jacinto Blvd., Austin TX 78712; (512) 471-4602.

TEXAS A&M UNIVERSITY AGGIES / KYLE FIELD

Website: https://12thman.com

Contact: 756 Houston St., College Station TX 77843; (888) 992-4443.

SOUTHERN METHODIST UNIVERSITY MUSTANGS / GERALD J. FORD STADIUM

Website: https://smumustangs.com

Contact: 5800 Ownby Dr., Dallas TX 75205.

UTAH

When it comes to Utah, there are some breathtaking places to see. Let's start with the Arches National Park where you'll see more than 2,000 natural stone arches, including the stunning Delicate Arch. Then there's Moab, with its red cliffs and mountains. But let's get to the sports.

UTAH JAZZ / VIVINT SMART HOME ARENA

The NBA's Utah Jazz have won nine division titles, but no championships yet. That's okay, because I said it before and I'll say it again, the best part about sports travel is just getting to see a professional team play and being part of the excitement and action. Not every team is going to have a winning record or amazing history. Right now the Jazz play at Vivint Smart Home Arena in Salt Lake City.

Website: https://www.nba.com/jazz/ and www.vivintarena.com

Contact: Vivint Smart Home Arena, 301 W South Temple, Salt Lake City UT 84101; (801) 325-2000.

UTAH OLYMPIC PARK

The Winter Olympics are spectacular, and the Utah Olympic Park is where some of the most incredible athletes have fought for the gold. Here you can take a one-hour tour and ride the shuttle bus to the top of the world's highest Nordic ski lifts. It's like the Olympics are right there; just use your imagination!

Website: https://utaholympiclegacy.org/location/utah-olympic-park

Info: The tours are offered 11 a.m, 1 p.m., and 3 p.m. Purchase tickets onsite, but call for availability first.

Contact: Utah Olympic Park, 3419 Olympic Pkwy., Park City UT 84098.

COLLEGE SPORTS TOUR

UTAH STATE UNIVERSITY AGGIES

The Utah State Aggies football team are conference champion winners—12 times, to be precise—and you should stop by and watch them play especially if it's against their rival BYU.

Website: https://utahstateaggies.com

Contact: Maverik Stadium, E 1000 N, Logan UT 84341.

BRIGHAM YOUNG UNIVERSITY COUGARS

Known as BYU, the Cougars' main rival is Utah State University. They play their football games at LaVell Edwards Stadium.

Website: https://byucougars.com

Contact: LaVell Edwards Stadium, 1700 N Canyon Rd., Provo UT 84604.

REAL SALT LAKE / RIO TINTO STADIUM

First, the pronunciation. If you didn't know it's not pronounced "reel" but "re-Al." The MLS soccer team has won the 2009 MLS Cup, and if you have a chance to watch them on the pitch, take it!

Website: https://www.rsl.com and https://riotintostadium.com

Contact: Rio Tinto Stadium, 9256 State St., Sandy UT 84070; (801) 727-2700.

VERMONT

Quick, when you think of Vermont, what's the first thing that comes to mind? If it isn't snow or skiing, you're wrong. That's the life of the state and when you're there, do as the Vermont residents do and take to the slopes. You should learn a bit about the state's skiing history at the museum and then support the local college sports teams. Then get back to the slopes.

COLLEGE SPORTS TOUR

UNIVERSITY OF VERMONT CATAMOUNTS / PATRICK GYM

The Catamounts basketball team works hard at getting to March Madness, winning the 2003, 2004, 2005, 2010, 2012, and 2017 America East Conference championships. The Catamounts play at Patrick Gym, which isn't too big—seating a bit more than 3,000 people—and doesn't offer tours like some of the larger stadiums do, but one of those seats can be yours if you plan ahead.

> **Website:** https://uvmathletics.com
>
> **Contact:** Patrick Gym, 97 Spear St., Burlington VT 05405; (802) 656-3131.

VERMONT SKI AND SNOWBOARD MUSEUM

In Stowe, in a small white building that looks like a little wedding chapel, sits the Vermont Ski and Snowboard Museum. Here you can see the history of skiing in Vermont. The exhibits rotate, so check the website before you go for the most current information.

> **Website:** https://www.vtssm.org
>
> **Info:** Suggested admission donation is $5 per adult.
>
> **Contact:** Vermont Ski and Snowboard Museum, 1 South Main St., Stowe VT 05672; (802) 253-9911.

VIRGINIA

Virginia is for lovers, right? That's what they say and that means sports lovers too, especially if you love college sports.

COLLEGE SPORTS TOUR

VIRGINIA POLYTECHNIC INSTITUTE AND STATE UNIVERSITY HOKIES / LANE STADIUM

Want to watch a football game in the stadium that's considered one of the loudest in the country? Then you're in the right place. ESPN even voted Lane Stadium number one in their "Top 20 Scariest Places to Play."

Website: https://hokiesports.com

Contact: Lane Stadium, 185 Beamer Way, Blacksburg VA 24060; (540) 231-6731

OLD DOMINION UNIVERSITY MONARCHS / CHARTWAY ARENA AT THE TED CONSTANT CONVOCATION CENTER

The Old Dominion Lady Monarchs basketball team represents Old Dominion University in Norfolk. They won two AIAW national championships in 1979 and 1980. Legendary players have included Nancy Lieberman and Anne Donovan. The team plays at Chartway Arena. Show them some love! Old Dominion's men's team has played in multiple NCAA tournaments and is also worth checking out.

Website: www.chartwayarena.com and www.odusports.com

Contact: Chartway Arena, 4320 Hampton Blvd., Norfolk VA 23508; (757) 683-4444.

Good Eats

Retired—and legendary—quarterback Joe Theismann became a restauranteur even before his playing days were over, so if you're in Virginia stop by his restaurant for a bite to eat. Enjoy some comfort food like mushroom meatloaf, beef stroganoff, burgers, or tacos.

WEBSITE: www.theismanns.com

CONTACT: Joe Theismann's Restaurant, 1800A Diagonal Rd., Alexandria VA; (703) 739-0777.

UNIVERSITY OF VIRGINIA CAVALIERS / JOHN PAUL JONES ARENA

As I was putting the finishing touches on this book, the Virginia Cavaliers took the NCAA basketball championship title. Wahoo! (That's also what they are known as!) They play at the John Paul Jones Arena.

> **Website:** https://virginiasports.com
>
> **Contact:** John Paul Jones Arena, 295 Massie Rd., Charlottesville VA 22903; (434) 243-4960.

VIRGINIA COMMONWEALTH UNIVERSITY RAMS / STUART C. SIEGEL CENTER

VCU reached the NCAA tournament a state record seven consecutive times from 2011 to 2017. Although the Cavaliers took the title last year, the VCU Rams deserve some support too. They play basketball at the Stuart C. Siegel Center.

> **Website:** www.siegelcenter.com
>
> **Contact:** Stuart C. Siegel Center, 1200 W Broad St., Richmond VA 23284; (804) 827-1000.
>
> **Did you know?** The Virginia Sports Hall of Fame and Museum is located at Virginia Beach Town Center where you can "Walk the Hall," a free pedestrian tour. It's all about Virginia sports and the athletes who have put the area on the map. For more information, visit https://vasportshof.com.

WASHINGTON

The Space Needle, Mount St. Helens, the Museum of Flight, and even the Gum Wall (where people have been putting their gum for years) are just some of the fun sights to see when you're in Washington. Of course, this is in between watching the Mariners, Seahawks, or Sounders play. Pick your sport of choice while you visit this incredible state.

SEATTLE MARINERS / T-MOBILE PARK

The MLB team plays at T-Mobile Park, which offers behind-the-scenes tours. Here you will go where the public doesn't boldly get to go, including the press box, owners suite, field, dugouts, visitors' clubhouse, All-Star Club, and more. The Seattle Mariners Hall of Fame is located with the Baseball Museum of the Pacific Northwest on the Main Concourse of T-Mobile Park, across from sections 135–141. It's a great way to see the history of the team and watch a game, all in the same visit.

Website: https://www.mlb.com/mariners

Info: During the offseason, January 14 to March 24 and in November and December, there are no tours on Monday and Wednesday. On Tuesday, the tours are offered at 10:30 a.m. and 12:30 p.m. On Friday and Saturday, they are offered at 10:30 a.m. and 12:30 p.m. On Sunday they are offered at 12:30 p.m. and 2:30 p.m. During the regular season, March 25–October, on game days with a game starting before 6 p.m., no tours are available. On game days with games starting after 6 p.m., there are tours at 10:30 a.m. and 12:30 p.m. On non-game days, tours are available at 10:30 a.m., 12:30 p.m., and 2:30 p.m.

Contact: T-Mobile Park, 1250 1st Ave. South, Seattle WA 98134; (206) 346-4000.

SEATTLE SEAHAWKS / CENTURYLINK FIELD

You too can be part of the "12th Fan"—the name that fans of the Seattle Seahawks have been given. I hope you're loud though, because those fans have set the Guinness World Record for the loudest crowd noise at a sporting event—not once, but twice. They did it against the San Francisco 49ers in September 2013, and again against the New Orleans Saints on Monday Night Football a few months later.

Website: https://www.seahawks.com and www.centurylinkfield.com

Info: From September 1 to May 31, the tour schedule is as follows: Monday through Thursday, no public tours. On Friday, Saturday, and Sunday, tours are offered at 10:30 a.m., 12:30 p.m., and 2:30 p.m. From June 1 to August 31, tours are offered seven days a week at 10:30 a.m., 12:30 p.m., and 2:30 p.m. Tickets *must* be purchased in person at the box office. Cost: adults (ages 12 and older), $14; seniors (ages 62 and older) and military, $10; children (ages 5–11), $8; children 4 and under, free.

Contact: CenturyLink Field, 800 Occidental Ave. South, Seattle WA 98134; (206) 381-7555.

The Seahawks play at CenturyLink Field, which offers 90-minute behind-the-scenes tours of the venue where you'll not only see the places in the stadium that others don't typically get to see, but your tour guide will show you views of Seattle, the Olympic Mountains, and Puget Sound, when it's a clear day of course.

SEATTLE SOUNDERS FC / CENTURYLINK FIELD

One of the most popular soccer teams in the country, the Sounders came into the league in 2009 and have won the US Open Cup four times, the Supporters' Shield in 2014, and the MLS Cup in 2016. In every season, they have qualified for the MLS Cup Playoffs.

The Sounders, along with the Seahawks, play at CenturyLink Field, which offers 90-minute behind-the-scenes tours of the venue.

Website: https://www.soundersfc.com and www.centurylinkfield.com

Info: From September 1 to May 31, the tour schedule is as follows: Monday through Thursday, no public tours. On Friday, Saturday, and Sunday, tours are offered at 10:30 a.m., 12:30 p.m., and 2:30 p.m. From June 1 to August 31, tours are offered seven days a week at 10:30 a.m., 12:30 p.m., and 2:30 p.m. Tickets *must* be purchased in person at the box office. Cost: adults (ages 12 and older), $14; seniors (ages 62 and older) and military, $10; children (ages 5–11), $8; children 4 and under, free.

Contact: CenturyLink Field, 800 Occidental Ave. South, Seattle WA 98134; (206) 381-7555.

COLLEGE SPORTS TOUR

UNIVERSITY OF WASHINGTON HUSKIES / HUSKY STADIUM

The Huskies are an impressive college football team—winning 17 conference championships, seven Rose Bowls, and two national championships recognized by the NCAA. They play at the aptly named Husky Stadium, which offers behind-the-scenes tours. You'll see the Husky Hall of Fame, walk down the football tunnel, and go onto the field. Keep in mind that tours require five business days notice and are not offered on holidays or weekends.

Website: https://gohuskies.com

Info: Tours are offered on Tuesday and Thursday at 2 p.m. Cost: A $10 per person donation to support the Competitive Edge Fund is suggested. No walk-ups allowed.

Contact: Husky Stadium, 3800 Montlake Blvd. NE, Seattle WA 98195; (206) 543-2210.

WASHINGTON STATE UNIVERSITY COUGARS / MARTIN STADIUM

Now for the Huskies' rivals—the Washington State University Cougars, who play at Martin Stadium. The two teams play in the annual Apple Cup, which started more than 120 years ago. The Huskies currently lead the series, which is typically played around Thanksgiving.

Website: https://wsucougars.com

Contact: Martin Stadium, 1775 NE Stadium Way, Pullman WA 99164; (509) 335-3564.

WEST VIRGINIA

West Virginia has extensive Civil War history, so there's a lot to see when you're in between games.

COLLEGE SPORTS TOUR

WEST VIRGINIA UNIVERSITY MOUNTAINEERS / WVU COLISEUM

Website: https://wvusports.com

Contact: WVU Coliseum, 3450 Monongahela Blvd., Morgantown WV 26505; (800) 988-4263.

MARSHALL UNIVERSITY THUNDERING HERD / JOAN C. EDWARDS STADIUM

You've heard the story and probably seen the movie, *We Are Marshall*; now it's time to see the team. But in case you haven't, it was 1970 when a plane crash took the lives of 75 of the school's football players, staff members, and boosters. The inspirational story of their comeback through grief and heartache is amazing. Now, while you're here, check out a game too. They play at Joan C. Edwards Stadium.

Website: https://herdzone.com/sports

Contact: Joan C. Edwards Stadium, 2001 3rd Ave., Huntington WV 25703.

WISCONSIN

It's known as America's Dairyland and is particularly famous for its cheese. When you get to Milwaukee, you'll see cheese, cheese, and cheese—and that's before you even get out of the airport! Seriously though, sports fans have plenty to see and do in the cheese state including baseball and, of course, the Green Bay Packers—sorry, I couldn't resist.

MILWAUKEE BREWERS / MILLER PARK

The Milwaukee Brewers were established in 1969 as the Seattle Pilots, but they quickly relocated and were named after the city's brew industry. They haven't been to the World Series since 1982. Announcing their games is the legendary Bob Uecker, who was also known for his appearance in the long-running television show *Mr. Belvedere*.

While you're taking in a game, make sure you walk the Miller Park Walk of Fame, located on the plaza area outside the ballpark where you can see home plate–shaped pieces of granite set in the ground to honor those who have been inducted. Miller Park offers tours of the dugouts, luxury suite level, visiting clubhouse, press box, Bob Uecker's broadcast booth, and more. There's also "The Selig Experience," which tells the story of Bud Selig's role in saving Major League Baseball in Milwaukee.

Website: https://www.mlb.com/brewers

Info: Classic Ballpark Tour pricing: adults, $15; youth, seniors, and military, $10. Tours do not take place when there is an afternoon home game or when special events are happening. Visit the website for the tour calendar.

Contact: Miller Park, 1 Brewers Way, Milwaukee WI 53214; (414) 902-4400.

MILWAUKEE BUCKS / FISERV FORUM

The legendary b-baller Kareem Abdul-Jabbar played for the Bucks for six seasons. They play in Fiserv Forum, where you can take in a 90-minute behind-the-scenes tour where you'll learn about this NBA franchise's history and the sports history of Milwaukee.

Website: https://www.fiservforum.com

Info: Cost: adults (ages 18 and older), $15; youth, seniors, and military, $12; children under 2, free. Visit their website for times and dates.

Contact: Fiserv Forum, 1111 Vel R. Phillips Ave., Milwaukee WI 53203; (414) 227-0504.

GREEN BAY PACKERS / LAMBEAU FIELD

If you read the intro to this book, you'll know that stepping on Lambeau Field was a bucket list dream of mine. These are "my boyzzzz" as I call them, and whether you love them or hate them, the Green Bay Packers stadium is worth a visit. They are owned by the community and won the very first Super Bowl in 1967. The Stadium is amazing, the tour is fantastic, and the gift shop is as big as a department store. Maybe I'm biased, but even my New York Giants–lovin' significant other absolutely had a blast. See the sidebar for things you must do while you're here.

✎ LISA'S PICK ✎
GREEN BAY, WISCONSIN

It's obvious that not every Green Bay Packers fan resides in Titletown, USA, but every week during football season, fans from around the country trek to America's Dairyland to see a game.

If you're one of those die-hard cheeseheads who are traveling to Wisconsin for one of the Green Bay Packers home games, here are eight things you must see and do while you're visiting:

Lambeau Field: Some fans skip the guided tour of this magnificent stadium because they figure they are going to Lambeau Field for the game anyway, but truly don't miss it. Lambeau Field has been the home field of the 13-time champion Green Bay Packers for 59 years, replacing City Stadium at East High School (which still exists and has a plaque that honors the franchise). Get your tickets early because they do sell out. On the Classic Tour, you will enter private suites, walk (or run if

That's me with Ej Garr, standing outside Lambeau Field in Green Bay. Best night of my life!
AUTHOR PHOTO

you wish) through the player's tunnel, and stand on the sidelines. You will also go to the top of the stadium and yell a resounding "Go Pack Go" to hear it echo back at you.

Website: https://www.packers.com/lambeau-field/stadium-tours

Cost: There's a Champions Tour, Classic Tour, Hall of Fame Tour, and more, so your cost is going to depend on what tour you buy. The Classic Tour tickets range from $9 to $15 per person.

Biggest Trophy Ever: Enter the stadium from the front and you won't miss the whopping 50-foot chrome Vince Lombardi Trophy replica. It weighs 14.5 tons and is two stories tall.

Hall of Fame: Also located inside Lambeau Field is 15,000 square feet of Green Bay Packers history. Listen to Brett Favre's Hall of Fame speech and watch game clips. Take photos next to the actual Lombardi trophies and see the uniforms that players actually wore during certain games.

Eat and Drink: Want to hang out with other Green Bay Packers fans? Stop at some of the popular venues, such as Titletown Brewing Company and 1919 Kitchen and Tap, for some good food and drinks, and soak up some pregame excitement. Don't forget to try deep fried cheese curds, a Wisconsin favorite. Websites: https://www.titletownbrewing.com; https://www.1919kitchenandtap.com

Lambeau Leap! No, you can't do the real Lambeau leap, but there is a mock wall outside of the stadium where you can pretend that you scored the winning touchdown!

Heritage Trail Tour: If you can't get enough of the Packers—and what fan can—check out the Heritage Trail Tour, a self-guided walk with exhibits, plaques, and statues that share the team story and how the residents of Green Bay came together to save a team from going completely bankrupt. Website: www.packersheritagetrail.com

Shop Till You Drop: Save some room in your suitcase because at the Packers Pro Shop, located inside Lambeau Field, you'll find everything under the sun that has a Packers logo—and I mean *everything*. You didn't even know that you needed those Green Bay Packers spices, did you? Website: https://www.packersproshop.com

Tailgate: It's game time! Get to the stadium early enough to throw around a football, chat it up, and make once-in-a-lifetime memories. There's nothing like tailgating with thousands of Packers fans.

There's so much that goes on during the game, but out-of-state Packers fans should make the most of the trip and visit the town before opening kickoff. Then, it's time to scream!

Did you know? The legendary Vince Lombardi–the Green Bay Packers coach from 1959 to 1967–died on September 3, 1970, and is buried at Mount Olivet Cemetery in Middletown, New Jersey, close to where he coached high school football.

COLLEGE SPORTS TOUR

University of Wisconsin Badgers / Camp Randall Stadium

The Green Bay Packers aren't the only football team in Wisconsin. The Wisconsin Badgers play in the Big 10 at Camp Randall Stadium, the fourth-oldest stadium in college football—built in 1917. Show them some love too while you're visiting this great state.

Website: https://uwbadgers.com

Contact: Camp Randall Stadium, 1440 Monroe St., Madison WI 53711; (608) 262-1866.

NFL Superfan Rides 25,000 Miles to Glory

Did you ever want to just throw your belongings in a bus and drive to every NFL stadium in the country? Sounds like a bucket list trip of a lifetime, and Rhett Grametbauer did it. As he says in the beginning of his documentary film, *25,000 Miles to Glory*, he just got tired of saying "Wouldn't it be great if . . ." and just decided that it was time to live out his dream.

As someone who couldn't wait to step on Lambeau Field—that was my bucket list dream—I had to watch this movie. I love people who go out and make their dreams come true.

It also reminds me of when I was co-hosting Sports Palooza Radio and had the opportunity to talk to Mac Engel about his book *Pigskin Rapture*. Mac talked to us about his trip to see four football games in Texas in four days. *Pigskin Rapture: Four Days in the Life of Texas Football* captures not just the action on the field, but all of the the sights, sounds, and smells of a state smitten with football: from KD's Bar-B-Q in Midland, to the rarefied air of Cowboys owner Jerry Jones's private box in AT&T Stadium. (Contact: KD's Bar-B-Q, 3109 Garden City Hwy., Midland TX 79701; https://kdsbarbq.com)

Grametbauer takes this idea much, much further. He drove his 1967 VW Bus, "Hail Mary," to all 31 NFL stadiums in 16 weeks to meet the fans and decide what makes them tick.

25,000 Miles to Glory is a fun documentary, and you'll get the feeling that you just want to jump right in the van and join them (what football fan wouldn't?!).

Don't think that this is a documentary about some rich dude who blew his inheritance on the trip of a lifetime. Sometimes he and his friends slept in the van because they didn't have a place to stay. He didn't just stop at each stadium, see a game, and move forward. He talked to fans at every stadium, including Donald "Dapper Don" Bartz, a well-known Buffalo Bills fan, as well as Bills fan "Pinto Ron" and New York Giants fan Joe "License Plate Guy" Ruback. He got to know each team's fandom at the tailgating parties. It's awesome hearing the stories about the fans and their craziness for their team.

Grametbauer meets up with other fans who have done the sports fan road trips, including four New York Jets fans—Anthony Mills, Angelo Fiouris, Mike Deissig, and Paul Kulciochetto—who met each other on Craigslist for a football road trip to the 2009 AFC Championship Game in Indianapolis, Indiana.

Of course, I think he didn't devote as much time to Lambeau Field and the Packers' fans as he could have, but I'm biased. But it is true that Green Bay, Wisconsin, revolves around the Packers' games.

The journey wasn't without its troubles, with a broken-down Volkswagen (actually a few times) and seriously cold weather in Minnesota, but they didn't stop.

Grametbauer has also written a book about the experience, also entitled *25,000 Miles to Glory*. He also started Foam Finger Nation to help dislocated sports fans find other fans of their favorite teams around the world and give them a medium to exchange fan experiences, road trip reviews, and recommendations.

In his book, he writes:

> Before buying Hail Mary [the car] I was clinging to a monotonous, regimented, mundane existence of being relegated to a nobody. My uninspired life was not what I had signed up for or dreamed about as a child, and I was determined more than ever to do something substantial with my life; to make something happen and to fulfill those promises and dreams I had as a child.

(This was written when the car had no brakes and was careening down a hill, out of control.)

The film *25,000 Miles to Glory* premiered at the Palace Theater in Canton, Ohio, during Hall of Fame weekend in 2016 and is available on several view-on-demand platforms.

You can learn more about Rhett at his website, www.RhettGrametbauer.com.

FANTASY CAMPS

Take your sports travel one step further and become a part of the team—not literally, but at these fantasy camps you can live out your dream of being a professional ballplayer, hockey player, football star, or soccer king. Skill doesn't matter. Put on your favorite team's uniform and play baseball, football, hockey, or basketball with current and former players. Trust me, it's a trip you'll never forget.

Typically these camps are held at the site of the team's training camps or centers and last anywhere from five to seven days. Keep in mind that some adult fantasy camps have minimum age restrictions. I've tried to list as many camps as possible, but always check the websites for the most up-to-date information. And if you don't see your favorite team listed here, just search the internet with the keywords "Fantasy Camp" and your favorite team's name.

For example, the New York Yankees are just one of many Major League Baseball teams that host fantasy camps, giving participants the opportunity to don the pinstripes, meet current and/or former players and coaches, and take the field. The camp is held at their spring training field in Tampa, Florida. The Yankees offer several camp options, including a men's camp (at press time the price was $5,299 per person for a week) held in November and January, women's mini-camp ($2,250 per person for four days and typically held in January), and a family fantasy clinic ($2,950 for three days). (Note: The family fantasy camp was sold out for November 2019 and, as of press date, the 2020 dates had not been listed.) For more information, visit https://www.mlb.com/yankees/fans/fantasy-camp.

Hey, we haven't forgotten about the kiddies. Many of these teams offer youth camps too!

Here is a probably-not-complete list of some adult sports fantasy camp experiences. These are the 2020 links, so if you can't go, you can always check back to see if they've updated the site for future years. Some teams offer fantasy camps every year, while some offer them every other year. For some, the camp is a one-time opportunity.

MAJOR LEAGUE BASEBALL

ARIZONA DIAMONDBACKS

The Diamondbacks' 2020 fantasy camp took place in January 2020 and included hotel accommodations, ground transportation, authentic jerseys, daily catered breakfast and lunch, an end-of-camp awards banquet, and more. The Diamondbacks require their attendees to be at least 30 years old. Their fantasy camp is held at Salt River Fields at Talking Stick in Arizona. For more information on the 2021 camp visit https://www.mlb.com/dbacks/academy/camps/fantasy.

ATLANTA BRAVES

If you're a Braves fan, then sign up for the fantasy camp that typically takes place in January of each year at CoolToday Park in North Port, Florida. The 2020 alumni included Sid Bream, Steve Avery, Denny Neagle, Mike Bielecki, Matt Diaz, Marvin Freeman, Pete Smith, and Marquis Grissom and such instructors as Bobby Cox, Tom Glavine, John Smoltz, Terry Pendleton, Dale Murphy, Bob Horner, and David Justice. The 2020 camp price started at $5,199 per person. For more information, visit atlanta.braves.mlb.com/atl/fan_forum/fantasycamp.jsp?c_id=atl.

BALTIMORE ORIOLES

Located in Sarasota, Florida, the 2020 Baltimore Orioles fantasy camp was held in January and included Mike Bordick, Al Bumbry, Rick Dempsey, Mike Devereaux, Chris Hoiles, Scott McGregor, and Orioles legend Jim Palmer. For more information, visit https://www.mlb.com/orioles/fans/dream-week.

BOSTON RED SOX

The Boston Red Sox fantasy camp also took place in January 2020 and included training at the official Red Sox spring training complex at JetBlue Park, which is also a replica of Fenway Park. In 2020, the camp coaches included Luis Tiant, Mike Timlin, Trot Nixon, Bill Mueller, and Rich Gedman. The cost was $5,299. For more information, visit https://www.mlb.com/redsox/fans/fantasy-camps/red-sox-fantasy-camp.

CHICAGO CUBS

By September 2019 the 2020 Chicago Cubs fantasy camp—held from January 26 to February 2, 2020—was already sold out, so keep an eye on the site now if you want to grab a spot for the 2021 camp. The cost was $4,995 based on hotel double occupancy with another camper. There was an additional fee for a single room. For more information, visit http://cubsfantasycamp.com.

CINCINNATI REDS

Reds Fantasy Camp is held in Goodyear, Arizona. You can sign up if you're 28 and attending with a family member, and ages 30 and older are eligible to pitch. The 2020 cost for new campers was $4,850, which includes a uniform: white pants, red/white jersey tops, undershirt, belt, socks, and cap. For more information, visit https://www.mlb.com/reds/fans/fantasy-camp-accommodations.

CLEVELAND INDIANS

Cleveland Indians Fantasy Camp is held at the team's new training facility in Goodyear, Arizona, and all proceeds benefit Cleveland Indians Charities. By September there was a waitlist for the 2020 camp, so check the website (https://www.mlb.com/indians/fans/fantasy-camp) frequently for the next camp openings.

COLORADO ROCKIES

Like almost all of the other MLB fantasy camps, the Colorado Rockies fantasy camp takes place at the end of January, so the 2020 fun is all done. When you sign up for the next available camp, you'll enjoy five days and four nights of hotel accommodations, personalized Rockies uniforms, daily camp collectibles, and personalized baseball cards (because who hasn't dreamed of their faces on a baseball card?). For more information, visit https://www.mlb.com/rockies/fans/fantasy-camp.

DETROIT TIGERS

At the 2020 fantasy camp, attendees got to play ball with members of the 1968 and 1984 world champion Tigers along with other former players in Lakeland, Florida. The camp includes hotel accommodations, personalized authentic home and away Tigers uniforms (yours to keep), pre-camp batting practice at Comerica Park, games in Tigertown, and so much more. For more information, visit https://www.mlb.com/tigers/fans/fantasy-camp/packages.

KANSAS CITY ROYALS

And you can be a Royal, it can run in your blood, at least at the Royals Fantasy Camp in Surprise, Arizona. For one week—the 2020 package cost $4,000—you will get personalized uniforms, professional coaching in hitting, fielding, pitching, and game fundamentals, an autograph session with alumni, and more. Visit https://www.mlb.com/royals/fans/fantasy-camp for more information.

LOS ANGELES DODGERS

Those who attended the Dodgers fantasy baseball camp in the past have been coached by such alumni as Steve Garvey, Andre Ethier, Eric Karros, Steve Sax, Steve Yeager, Manny Mota, Kevin Gross, Ken Landreaux, and Bob Geren. At Camelback Ranch in Arizona, the cost of the 2020 camp was $4,995. For more information, visit https://www.mlb.com/camelback-ranch/fantasy-camp.

MILWAUKEE BREWERS

Celebrate the newly renovated Maryvale Stadium by spending a week in sunny Arizona! For $4,899, Brewers fans made their baseball fantasy a reality. Coaches included Ken Sanders, Jerry Augustine, Greg Vaughn, Jeff Cirillo, Jim Gantner, Scott Karl, J. J. Hardy, Corey Hart, Tim Dillard, and Ed Sedar. There was also a special appearance by the legendary Rollie Fingers. As with most teams, they offer a waiting list if you missed the signups, so visit https://www.mlb.com/mariners/fans/fantasy-camp for more information.

MINNESOTA TWINS

The 2020 Minnesota Twins Baseball Fantasy Camp was held in Fort Myers, Florida, and first-timers cost $4,795. At camp attendees met alumni including Frank Viola, Rod Carew, and Bert Blyleven. For more information, visit http://yuratwin.com/twins-fantasy-camp-info/register-now.php.

NEW YORK METS

Let's Go Mets! We can't help them to win a World Series, but fans can don a uniform and play some games with the alumni to improve their skills. The camp includes accommodations, two personalized, authentic Mets uniforms, the awards dinner with the pros, daily games, and more. Camp is approximately $4,300. Find out more information at https://www.mlb.com/mets/fans/fantasy-camp/frequently-asked-questions.

OAKLAND A'S

Join a group of A's alumni and fellow baseball fans each January at the A's training facility in Mesa, Arizona. The camp offers a gold and a green package (length of accommodations vary) and a tag-along package for those family members or best friends who want to watch, but not play. For more information, visit https://www.mlb.com/athletics/fans/fantasy-camp.

PHILADELPHIA PHILLIES PHANTASY BASEBALL CAMP

You'll love the fun at the Phillies Phantasy Baseball Camp in Clearwater, Florida. In 2020, campers met Larry Bowa, Jim Thome, Ricky Jordan, Dickie Noles, and other Phillies alumni. The all-inclusive price includes three options for camp—you can be a player, general manager, or a Phan and cheer on a player (21+ to be a Phan). Costs in 2020 were $4,995 for a camper, $4,200 to be a general manager, and $1885 to be a Phan. For more information, visit https://www.philliesphantasycamp.com/pages/details.html.

PITTSBURGH PIRATES

Over in Bradenton, Florida, the spring training site of the Pirates, you can become part of their fantasy camp, which includes your own Pirates jersey, a clubhouse locker for the week, a big-league baseball card, and so much more. Sign up early or end up on a waiting list because these camps sell out quickly. For more information, visit https://www.mlb.com/pirates/fans/fantasy-camp.

SAN DIEGO PADRES

The San Diego Padres hosted their second-annual Padres Fantasy Camp at the Peoria Sports Complex in Arizona in 2020. Notable Padres alumni and current members of the minor-league coaching staff who attended included Trevor Hoffman, Randy Jones, Wally Joyner, Tony Gwynn Jr., Mark "Mud" Grant, and Andy Ashby. For more information on future camps, visit https://www.mlb.com/padres/fans/fantasy-camp.

SAN FRANCISCO GIANTS

Most of the camps are held in January, but the Giants hold their camp in March. Most of the camps are held for ages 30 and up, but the Giants camp is for ages 25 and up. They have also offered a two-day fantasy camp. For more information on both, visit https://www.mlb.com/giants/fans/fantasy-camp.

SEATTLE MARINERS

In 2020, the Seattle Mariners held their inaugural fantasy camp at the Peoria Sports Complex, their spring training home in Arizona. Participants received uniforms and were coached on the fundamentals of pitching, hitting, fielding, and baserunning by Mariners alumni and members of the organization's coaching staff. The week culminated with playoffs and a championship game (bragging rights!). For more information, visit https://www.mlb.com/mariners/fans/fantasy-camp.

HOCKEY

DETROIT RED WINGS

This NHL team hosts an exclusive fantasy camp to give attendees three days on and off the ice at Little Caesars Arena with their favorite Hockeytown legends, such as former Red Wings players Larry Murphy, Kirk Maltby, Darren McCarty, and Dallas Drake. The camp was held in 2019 at the Belfor Training Center—and was sold out—but as of press time was not announced for 2020. For more information, visit https://www.nhl.com/redwings/fans/fantasy-camp.

MARIO LEMIEUX FANTASY HOCKEY CAMP

The Mario Lemieux Fantasy Hockey Camp is a fund-raising event run by the Mario Lemieux Foundation. Campers are divided into four teams and Mario Lemieux rotates from team to team during the round-robin tournament play, so you're guaranteed to play with and against Mario at least once. You'll also receive Pittsburgh Penguins and Mario Lemieux Fantasy Hockey Camp branded equipment and apparel. Camp games are held at PPG Paints Arena, the home of the Pittsburgh Penguins, and at the UPMC Lemieux Sports Complex, the Penguins' practice facility. In addition to Lemieux himself, players and coaches from previous camps have included Paul Coffey, Bryan Trottier, Chris Chelios, Joe Mullen, Bernie Nicholls, Grant Fuhr, Tie Domi, Curtis Joseph, Jay Caufield, Mark Recchi, Bill Guerin, Kevin Stevens, Gary Roberts, Larry Murphy, Theo Fleury, Rick Tocchet, Alexei Kovalev, Pierre Turgeon, Ron Duguay, Sergei Gonchar, Michel Goulet, Colby Armstrong, Clark Gillies, Pierre Larouche, Randy Hillier, Eddie Johnston, and Mike Eruzione. This camp is quite pricey—pricing for the 2019 camp was $13,266 for a new camper, $12,766 for a returning camper, $7,566 for a goalie, and $3,866 for a guest. Campers need to be 21 years old. This camp has an extensive waiting list, so if you're interested, visit https://mariolemieux.org/our-events/mario-lemieux-fantasy-hockey-camp.

PHILADELPHIA FLYERS

In 2019, the Flyers offered their fifth edition of the Flyers Alumni Fantasy Camp in Atlantic City, New Jersey. Attendees with various levels of hockey skills and playing experience played games and were instructed by Flyers alumni, including Mark Howe, Bill Barber, Danny Briere, Keith Jones, Brad Marsh, Bob "the Hound" Kelly, Joe Watson, and Ian Laperrière. Proceeds from the Flyers Alumni Fantasy Camp benefit the Flyers Alumni Association. Early registration is highly recommended.

Previous camps have sold out all registration spots. For more information, visit www
.flyersalumni.org/fantasy-camp.

SAN JOSE SHARKS

In 2019, the Sharks Alumni Foundation created a weekend hockey experience, held
in April. Teams registered and played games and enjoyed having trainers, skate sharp-
eners, massage therapists, and your own locker room as part of the experience. Bags,
jerseys, and socks were also included. For 2020 dates and prices, visit https://sharks
alumnifoundation.org/sharksalumnifantasycamp.

BASKETBALL

JIM BOEHEIM FANTASY BASKETBALL CAMP

For three days, you too can experience the Jim Boeheim Fantasy Basketball Camp.
It's limited to ages 35+ and is limited to 40 men. You will have the opportunity to
run the same drills, offensive and defensive sets, team practices, and game analytics
used by the Syracuse men's basketball team. For 2020 and future dates, visit https://
boeheimfoundation.org/sports/2018/1/29/jim-boeheims-fantasy-camp.aspx.

JOHN CALIPARI BASKETBALL FANTASY CAMP EXPERIENCE

John Calipari has been head coach of the University of Kentucky men's team since
2009. If you want to play ball under his tutelage, sign up for the John Calipari
Basketball Fantasy Camp Experience, which has been held for the past eight years.
Packages start at $7,495, and you can find more information and future dates at
www.johncaliparibasketballexperience.com.

K ACADEMY

Want to experience what it's like to play Duke Basketball? The K Academy has been
around for 17 years. Campers spend five days in Cameron Indoor Stadium where
you go from opening day tryouts to a championship tournament. Play games on
Coach K Court in Cameron and learn the inside scoop on Duke's five-time national
championship program. K Academy tuition is $10,000 and you must be age 35 or
older. For more information, visit https://kacademy.com.

NFL

KANSAS CITY CHIEFS

The Chiefs held their sixth annual fantasy camp in 2019. Since it's been a regular
thing, check their website for 2020 dates and beyond. The one-day camp was held
in May and cost $2,000. Fans were broken down into groups and drills were led
by former Chiefs players, including Pro Football Hall of Fame offensive guard Will
Shields, and Hall of Famer Jan Stenerud teaching campers how to kick a field goal.
For more information, visit https://www.chiefs.com/fans/fantasycamp.

NEW ENGLAND PATRIOTS

Experience a day in the life of a Patriots player at the Patriots Fantasy Camp, where you will also receive exclusive access to all of the Patriots' training facilities and their coaching staff. All proceeds from this charitable event support the efforts of the New England Patriots Foundation. The dates for 2020 have not been announced yet. Visit https://www.patriots.com/photos/fans-go-behind-the-scenes-at-patriots-fantasy-camp#5de49c61-a6e9-4fd5-b826-1f685cbf608c for more information.

PITTSBURGH STEELERS

At the 2019 Steelers Men's Fantasy Camp event, attendees met Pro Football Hall of Famers and Steelers Hall of Honor inductees Dermontti Dawson and Rod Woodson. The weekend event was held in May and included dorm housing (two per room), meals, and a black Steelers Nike replica jersey. The 2019 price was $799. For more information on future camps visit https://www.steelers.com/schedule/event-calendar/mens-fantasy-camp.

SOCCER

LA GALAXY

The Galaxy ran a three-day fantasy soccer camp in September 2019 that included a customized LA Galaxy uniform and three days of training by former LA Galaxy players, access to locker room and training facilities, lunch with the coaching staff and players, tickets to a home match, and more. The cost is $1,025 per person, but check the website for future dates and prices. Visit https://youth.lagalaxy.com/camps.

SEATTLE SOUNDERS

Have you always wanted to play on the pitch? You can at the Sounders FC fantasy camp, where you experience an exclusive behind-the-scenes look at what it's like to be a Sounders FC player and meet technical staff, interact with alumni, and receive quality training from the first team, S2, and Academy coaches. Held at the Starfire Sports Complex, the home training ground of Sounders FC, you'll get to have a photo op with your favorite players too. For prices and future camp dates, visit https://www.soundersfc.com/camps/adult_camp.

RESOURCES

Here is the Tourism Bureau for every state. Check with each state before your vacation for information, events, savings, and more.

Alabama: https://alabama.travel; (800) 252-2262
Alaska: www.travelalaska.com; (800) 862-5275
Arizona: www.visitarizona.com; (866) 275-5816, (602) 364-3700
Arkansas: www.arkansas.com; (501) 682-6900
California: www.visitcalifornia.com; (916) 444-4429
Colorado: www.colorado.com; (800) COLORADO
Connecticut: www.ctvisit.com; (888) CTVISIT, (888) 288-4748
Delaware: www.visitdelaware.com; (866) 284-7483
Florida: www.visitflorida.com/en-us.html (888) 735-2872
Georgia: www.exploregeorgia.org; (800) VISITGA
Hawaii: www.hawaiitourismauthority.org; (808) 539-3428
Idaho: https://visitidaho.org; (208) 334-2470
Illinois: www.enjoyillinois.com; (312) 814-4732
Indiana: https://visitindiana.com; (800) 677-9800
Iowa: www.traveliowa.com; (515) 348-6245
Kansas: www.travelks.com; (785) 296-2009
Kentucky: www.kentuckytourism.com; (502) 564-4930, (800) 225-8747
Louisiana: www.louisianatravel.com; (800) 677-4082
Maine: https://visitmaine.com; (888) 624-6345; (207) 624-7483
Maryland: www.visitmaryland.org; (866) 639-3526
Massachusetts: www.massvacation.com; (617) 973-8500
Michigan: www.michigan.org; (888) 784-7328
Minnesota: www.exploreminnesota.com; (888) VISITMN; (651) 556-8465
Mississippi: https://visitmississippi.org; (601) 359-3297
Missouri: www.visitmo.com; (573) 751-4133
Montana: www.visitmt.com; (800) 847-4868
Nebraska: https://visitnebraska.com; (402) 471-3796
Nevada: https://travelnevada.com; (800) NEVADA8
New Hampshire: www.visitnh.gov/; (603) 271-2665
New Jersey: www.visitnj.org; (800) VISITNJ, (609) 599-6540
New Mexico: www.newmexico.org; (505) 827-7400, (505) 827-7336
New York: www.iloveny.com; (800) 225-5697
North Carolina: www.visitnc.com; (800) VISITNC
North Dakota: www.ndtourism.com; (800) 435-5663, (701) 328-2525
Ohio: https://ohio.org; (800) BUCKEYE
Oklahoma: www.travelok.com; (800) 652-6552
Oregon: www.traveloregon.com; (800) 547-7842

Pennsylvania: https://visitpa.com; (800) 847-4872

Rhode Island: www.visitrhodeisland.com/; (401) 278-9100

South Carolina: https://discoversouthcarolina.com; (803) 734-0124

South Dakota: www.travelsouthdakota.com; (800) 732-5682

Tennessee: www.tnvacation.com; (615) 741-2159

Texas: www.traveltexas.com; (512) 463-2000

Utah: https://utah.com; (801) 356-9077

Vermont: https://www.vermontvacation.com; (800) 837-6668 (Vacation Planning Information); (802) 828-3237 (Main Line)

Virginia: www.virginia.org; (804) 545-5600

Washington: www.experiencewa.com; (800) 544-1800

West Virginia: https://wvtourism.com; (800) CALLWVA

Wisconsin: www.travelwisconsin.com; (800) 432-8747

Wyoming: www.travelwyoming.com; (800) 225-5996

SITE INDEX

ABOUT THE AUTHOR

Lisa Iannucci is a professional writer, founder of "The Virgin Traveler," and host of her *Reel Travels* podcast (blogtalkradio.com/reeltravels). She has been a regular contributor to TravelPulse.com and has written travel articles for the *Los Angeles Times*, Content That Works, the *Poughkeepsie Journal*, and other publications. She contributes film/TV articles to ReelLifeWithJane.com and FF2Media.com and has interviewed hundreds of celebrities. She has coauthored 17 books on a wide variety of topics, including biographies of Will Smith and Ellen DeGeneres. She lives with her family and five televisions in the Hudson Valley, New York area.